Selecting the President

SELECTING THE PRESIDENT

The Nominating Process in
Transition

Howard L. Reiter

University of Pennsylvania Press
Philadelphia

Copyright © 1985 by the University of Pennsylvania Press

Library of Congress Cataloging in Publication Data

Reiter, Howard L.
  Selecting the president.

  Bibliography: p.
  Includes index.
  1. Presidents—United States—Nomination.   I. Title.
JK521.R45   1985   324.5'6   85-8555
ISBN 0-8122-7990-5 (alk. paper)
ISBN 0-8122-1217-7 (pbk. : alk. paper)

Printed in the United States of America

To my parents

Contents

List of Figures

List of Tables

Acknowledgments

O ne's first book comes at the end of a long funnel of scholarly causation, and I was lucky to learn about political parties and the electoral process from five distinguished gentlemen, Samuel Beer, Seymour Martin Lipset, Theodore Lowi, H. Douglas Price, and Allan Sindler. They directed me toward asking the right questions, and I hope I have followed their example in pursuing answers. The usual disclaimer about their lack of responsibility for my errors applies with particular force here, as this study was not an outgrowth of any student project.

Five friends and colleagues read an earlier draft of the entire manuscript and tried to improve it. They were John Beer, James Ceaser, Akira Hayama, Theodore Lowi, and W. Wayne Shannon. For their help and patience I am grateful. An earlier version of the first part of Chapter 5 appeared in the *American Politics Quarterly* 8 (July 1980): 303–318, and acknowledges the help of Walter Dean Burnham, H. Douglas Price, David RePass, and Richard Styskal. Portions of this book are a revised version of my paper "The Irrelevance of Reform," presented to the 1985 annual meeting of the American Politics Group in Great Britain and one of the Essex Papers in Politics and Government at the University of Essex. A similar paper, entitled "The Limitations of Reform," is to be published in the *British Journal of Political Science*, probably in October 1985.

This study would not have been possible without the support of the staff of the Institute for Social Inquiry at the University of Connecticut, headed by my colleague Everett Ladd, as well as the University of Connecticut Research Foundation. My longtime good friend Kathleen Frankovic of CBS News and her efficient staff provided data instantly and graciously whenever I needed any. The final version of the manuscript was completed during a term at the University of Essex in England, and the Government Department there under its chairman, Ivor Crewe, was most hospitable.

At the University of Pennsylvania Press, which belied the stereotype of the dilatory academic press, Janet Greenwood, Michael Hennelly, Jo Mugnolo, and Zachary Simpson were especially helpful, and Margaret Connolly provided crucial support at a time when it was necessary; to her I am especially indebted. Two anonymous reviewers will see their helpful suggestions reflected in the final version.

Finally, my wife Laura has shared in the ups and downs of this project, and just for being there has contributed mightily to it.

HOWARD L. REITER
Wivenhoe Park, England

ONE

Causes and Effects

Few political events in the United States stimulate as much interest as Presidential campaigns, and for good reason. The President is both chief executive and head of state of the West's leading power. He and his running-mate are the only public officials chosen (indirectly, to be sure) by the entire national electorate. The President is more than a political figure, for he is regarded by many as a potent symbol of the nation, and great hopes and expectations are projected onto him. Moreover, as the only nationwide election, the Presidential selection process provides a barometer of where the nation is and where it is going—the policies it will adopt, the groups that are emerging and those that are declining, and the national mood. Presidential campaigns not only stimulate higher voter turnout than any other elections but also attract enormous attention from the news media and from the academic community.

The process by which the major parties select their nominees for the White House seems far different today from what it was a generation ago. It has become commonplace to speak of a "revolution" or at least fundamental changes in that process, and not the least of the concerns of the political science profession has been, in the words of Pogo, "Does we gain or lose?" Every four years, politicians and journalists join the debate by applauding how open the process has become or decrying a system that seems to favor candidates of unbridled ambition or passionate intensity. Surely these are important matters.

My purpose in this study of the recent nominating process is to ascertain whether, and if so when and why, a new system has developed and to describe its contours. I have some answers in mind

1

and will present them with as much evidence as I can muster. But first I want to present my hypothesis in the context of what others have written, because reasonable men and women disagree about the answers to these questions. The authors whose explanations differ from mine will provide counterhypotheses and alternative models for which my data and arguments will have serious implications. After presenting my hypothesis, I will discuss how to go about testing it, providing examples of the methodological flaws to which others have been prone.

Four Causal Theories

The 1972 School

Perhaps the most prevalent theory is that the process has indeed changed and that the main causes are changes in the formal rules of the game. Specifically, in 1968 the Democratic national convention mandated what became known as the Commission on Party Structure and Delegate Structure or, more commonly, the McGovern-Fraser Commission.[1] That commission and its several successors made numerous changes in the way the nominating process was to be conducted. The rules and recommendations of the McGovern-Fraser Commission can be loosely grouped into three categories: (1) procedural fairness, including publication of party rules, uniform times and dates for delegate selection meetings, and abolition of high participation fees, (2) proportional representation for the followers of the various Presidential candidates, by way of abolition of the unit rule and the encouragement of proportional representation, and (3) the "reasonable" representation of women, young people, and members of racial minority groups. By the time of the 1972 convention, these guidelines had been adopted, and they enabled insurgents to challenge delegations that had been chosen oligarchically or with insufficient attention to demographic requirements. The Republicans adopted similar rules changes, but they were not as far-reaching or as long-lasting as the Democrats' changes.[2] One change that was initiated by the Democrats and did affect the Republican party was the McGovern-Fraser Commission's indirect encouragement of direct primaries to elect convention delegates. The number of such primaries soared in 1972 and rose sharply through 1980 (see Table 1.1).

TABLE 1.1. Number of states with delegate selection primaries, 1912–1984

Year	Democratic		Republican	
	Number of states	Percentage of convention votes	Number of states	Percentage of convention votes
1912	12	32.9	13	40.8
1916	20	53.5	20	58.9
1920	16	44.6	20	57.8
1924	15	43.7	18	53.6
1928	18	43.6	16	44.9
1932	17	41.2	14	37.7
1936	14	36.5	12	37.5
1940	13	35.8	13	38.8
1944	14	36.7	13	38.7
1948	14	36.3	12	36.0
1952	15	38.7	14	41.0
1956[a]	20	43.1	18	41.6
1960[b]	17	40.3	15	38.6
1964	13	36.9	15	42.4
1968[b]	14	38.7	14	37.1
1972[c]	21	56.1	18	46.0
1976[c]	27	61.5	26	57.5
1980[d]	34	76.5	35	76.7
1984[e]	29	66.5	24	53.8

[a] Includes Alaska and the District of Columbia.
[b] Includes the District of Columbia.
[c] Includes the District of Columbia for Democrats only.
[d] Includes the District of Columbia and Puerto Rico.
[e] Includes the District of Columbia and Puerto Rico for Democrats only.

According to some, these changes in the rules had a profound effect on the nominating process, the most significant change being the removal of control over the delegates from state and local party leaders. The most dramatic example of this was the ejection of Chicago's Mayor Richard Daley from the 1972 convention because he had not followed the McGovern-Fraser guidelines in composing his delegation. The primaries also seemed to hurt party leaders by enabling candidates to win delegates by ignoring the leaders and appealing directly to the voters.

The McGovern-Fraser reforms were followed by other Democratic reform commissions. Perhaps the most important of these to date was the Commission on Delegate Structure and Party Structure, or the Mikulski Commission, which tightened the proportional representation rules for the 1976 convention,[3] allegedly destroying the ability of party leaders to bring to conventions delegations that are united under their control. Again, the Republicans were affected by this change in many states because state laws dictating selection procedures were changed. Other significant Democratic efforts have included the Commission on Presidential Nomination and Party Structure or Winograd Commission, which mandated that half the delegates to the 1980 convention be women, and the Commission on Presidential Nomination or Hunt Commission, which increased the participation of party and public officials and relaxed some of the earlier reforms in anticipation of the 1984 convention (see Chapter 8).

Not long after the McGovern-Fraser rules went into effect, Congress got into the act by amending the 1971 Federal Election Campaign Act (FECA) in 1974. After the Supreme Court altered the resulting law in 1976, the FECA ended up providing matching federal funds to Presidential candidates during the primaries, requiring limits on contributions and (for those accepting the matching funds) expenditures and allocating funds to the major parties for running the conventions and to the major-party nominees for their postconvention campaigns. These reforms were expected to affect the nominating process in many ways, notably by making it easier for candidates of modest means to pay for their campaigns and to avoid becoming captives of wealthy contributors and special interests. Of course, they also affected the role of the party in the fundraising process.[4]

I am calling the scholars under discussion here the 1972 school, because they argue that these dramatic changes began with the 1972 Democratic convention. Most adherents to this school claim that the new rules were a grave mistake. None has been more prolific in assailing the alleged effects of these reforms than Austin Ranney, a former member of the McGovern-Fraser Commission.

His most stark statement of the impact of the new rules is that there has been

a series of events, still in train in 1976, by which the Democratic party made the most radical changes in procedures for choosing its presidential nominees since the 1820s, when national conventions replaced congressional caucuses as the nominating body. . . . The net result has been a major change in the nature of presidential politics and therefore in our whole political system.[5]

What was the nature of this change?

The rules make presidential nominees even less indebted than ever before to congressional and other national, state, and local party leaders and more indebted to the nominees' own candidate organizations and contributors and to the voters in the primaries. Hence presidents produced by such a system seem even less likely than ever before to succeed in—or even attempt—drives for party unity among presidentially-led congressional parties. The new reforms have also shifted the balance of power over presidential nominations from old-style party "brokers" to new-style issue and candidate enthusiasts. They have thereby stripped the old-style party leaders of most of their traditional ability to use the nominations as occasions for bargaining and compromise. And the new-style participants have little inclination to use their increased power for such purposes—which many of them regard as downright immoral.[6]

And Ranney has flatly stated that "Carter could only have been nominated under the present system and under the present rules in 1976."[7]

Allied with Ranney was another Democrat disturbed by the rules, Jeane Kirkpatrick, who called the reforms the most important cause of "party decomposition" and added, "It is almost impossible to overstate the impact of primaries on the nominating process."[8] When pressed by David Adamany as to whether parties had not begun to decline long before the rules changes, Kirkpatrick admitted that the reforms "have merely accelerated and contributed to" that decline, which seems to be a major concession in light of earlier rhetoric.[9] Others who have attributed important and deleterious consequences to the rules changes have been Edward Banfield, William Cavala, James Ceaser, Judith Center, Paul David,

James Davis, Nelson Polsby, Byron Shafer, and Stephen Wayne, as well as journalist David Broder and activists Penn Kemble and Josh Muravchik.[10] In the words of Kemble and Muravchik, "The reforms have left one of the major institutions of American democracy in a shambles."[11]

But there is no ideological homogeneity to the 1972 school, for it includes some who applaud what they see as the equally significant but salutary effects of the reforms. Writes William Crotty, "The reforms introduced a remarkable era to American politics. More was attempted, and accomplished, than can truthfully be said to have been envisioned in the decades since the Progressive movement of the early 1900s."[12] This was, says Crotty, "a revolution in party operations," for it opened the Democratic party while weakening the power of party leaders, nationalizing the party, and institutionalizing the rule of law.[13] Like Ranney, he sees Carter's nomination before 1972 as "unthinkable."[14] F. Christopher Arterton, Robert Nakamura, and Denis Sullivan share Crotty's perspective.[15]

Our concern here is not the disagreement between Ranney et al. and Crotty et al. but in the underlying consensus that unites all of them—the argument that the recent rules changes engendered a revolution of sorts in the nominating process. This causal model is depicted in Figure 1.1.

I should add that these authors and others of the 1972 school do occasionally qualify their position, but each has spent so much time criticizing or defending the reforms and attributing so many consequences to them that the qualifying statements pale in significance.

FIGURE 1.1. **Causal model of the 1972 school**

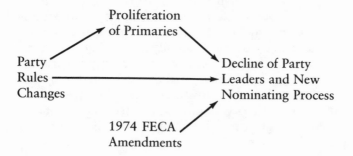

The Party-Decline School

Another group of scholars agrees with the 1972 school that the system has changed and essentially agrees as to which changes have occurred, but it presents a different causal model to explain this transformation. While not denying the importance of changes in the formal rules, these authors argue that the reforms were only part of a number of important developments that undercut the strength of party leaders. The decline of the political party in the United States is a phenomenon that has been studied for some time by many analysts, whether the focus has been on the tendency of voters to use partisanship as a guide to voting behavior less often than they used to, on the looser bonds of party among elected officials, or on the atrophy of party organization.[16] The causes of the decline of the party are said to be the advent of the mass media, civil service reforms and judicial decisions which undercut the patronage system, the rise of the educated middle class and assimilation of immigrants, government social welfare programs, new campaign techniques, and the nationalization of politics, which are said to have deprived the parties of their electoral base, their resources, and many of the functions they used to perform.

It is difficult to pinpoint the causes of such a complex set of phenomena or even the date of this decline. Walter Dean Burnham argues that it started as far back as the 1890s.[17] At some point, argues the party-decline school, these changes reached the stage when by almost any measure American political parties had declined in their effectiveness and impact on the rest of the political process. Several kinds of data suggest that the mid-1960s seem to have been that point.

Perhaps the most familiar indicator of the decline of partisanship is the proportion of the American electorate who identify themselves as independents. According to the surveys of the Center for Political Studies of the University of Michigan, from 1952 through 1964 that figure fluctuated from 19 percent to 23 percent. In 1966 it leaped to 28 percent, and it continued rising until from 1974 through 1980 it hovered around 37 percent. In 1982 it dipped to 30 percent. Only in 1966 did it grow more than 4 percent. The same timing occurred with regard to ticket-splitting. We can examine how people had voted for President and Congress. From 1952 to 1964, some 11 percent to 17 percent of respondents split their tickets in races for the Presidency and the Senate (not counting votes cast for third-party and independent candidates). In 1968 that figure rose to 19 percent and has exceeded 20 percent ever since. Similarly, in voting for President and Representative, the figure rose from 12 percent to 16 percent from 1952 to 1964, to 18 percent in 1968, and at least 25 percent ever since.[18]

Parties in Congress have declined in the same period and at roughly the same time. *Congressional Quarterly* defines a "party unity" vote as one in which a majority of Democrats vote one way and a majority of Republicans vote the other way. Since 1954, when the publication first began compiling statistics on these votes, the proportion of congressional votes that were party-unity votes has fluctuated. In both houses of Congress from the early 1960s until around 1970, the incidence of party-unity votes plummeted. We can pinpoint the greatest change by computing the means for every five-year period in the series and comparing adjacent series: the 1954–1958 mean compared with the 1959–1963 mean, 1955–1959 with 1960–1964, and so forth. The largest drops in the Senate means clustered around the years 1963–1964 and 1965–1966, and in the House around 1965–1966. Since the early 1970s, the rates for both houses have risen, more so in the Senate than in the House.

On these party-unity votes, how often has the mean member of Congress voted with his or her party? In both houses, there has been a consistent drop since 1954. For both parties in the House, the largest decline surrounded the years 1967–1968; for Senate Republicans the years were 1965–1966. Senate Democrats experienced their two largest declines in the late 1950s, but they were followed closely by the drop surrounding the years 1965–1966.[19]

For all the variations among these survey and congressional data, there is a consistent pattern: an unusual and often unequaled decline in the indicators of partisanship in the middle to late 1960s, more precisely during the Johnson administration. In addition, the 1964 Presidential election marked the first of the longest unbroken string of elections in which the turnout declined. Why the overt commitment of American voters and politicians to parties and elections should have diminished at that particular time is a matter of great speculation and some controversy. All in all, there is little evidence that the long-term phenomena to which the decline of partisanship has been attributed, such as civil service reforms or social welfare programs, reached the takeoff stage shortly before the mid-1960s. However, there is one exception—the rise of television. According to data compiled by the A. C. Nielsen Company, 1962 was the first year in which more than nine out of ten American households had a TV set, and the Roper survey found that in 1961 people were for the first time more likely to cite television as a more credible news source than any other medium. This suggests that the saturation of the American public by television may have affected the political system in many ways, not the least significant of which was the decline of partisanship.[20]

As suggestive as these data are, they are hardly conclusive, and it would be difficult if not impossible to establish that the advent of television was the most important precipitant of the weakening of partisanship. On the contrary, some of the trends discussed in this volume began before the heyday of television. One longitudinal study has shown that the mass media have been increasingly downplaying the role of parties in their reporting over time, but it is difficult to know whether these journalistic trends have affected public opinion, or vice versa.[21] For all the discussion of the influence of journalists on the nominating process, however, this book will be relatively little concerned with that role. I am trying to be rigorously empirical and will measure only those phenomena that are measurable. It is extremely difficult to test what is perhaps the most common allegation about media impact: the effect that journalists have when they judge that a candidate has run "better than expected" or "worse than expected." Is this proof of the disproportionate power of the media, or would *most* informed observers have concluded that, say, Edmund Muskie should have won the New Hampshire Democratic primary in 1972 by a larger margin than he did, or that John Anderson ran better in some of the primaries that he lost than anybody should reasonably have expected him to? If most informed observers would have concurred with the assessment of the media, it is difficult to conclude that journalists play an independent and disproportionate role.

Even if we were able to isolate the proximate causes of the decline of partisanship, the remote and underlying causes would not be easy to establish. Some authors have tried to place the decline of party within a context of broader social change. A number of analysts, notably those identified with neo-conservatism, stress the emergence of a so-called postindustrial society. If society can indeed best be understood as dominated by a "new class" of technological and intellectual elites rather than the capitalists who govern industrial society, this may be sufficient to understand why parties, and most of the political system, have undergone vast changes. In particular, the new elites are alleged to rely on their control of cultural symbols, notably in the mass media, higher education, and government, and therefore have fostered the decline of such institutions as parties that have represented other interests.[22] On the left, some have argued that the "crisis of late capitalism" has led political elites to centralize power in order to coordinate the survival of a beleaguered system. This in turn reduces the significance of popular institutions, such as parties.[23] It is beyond the purview of this volume to evaluate these or other theories that attempt to explain the decline of parties, but these theories do suggest that the phenomena under examination may reflect the most profound kinds of social changes.

Whatever the underlying or proximate causes, by the middle of the 1960s the process of party decline was apparently well under way. One consequence of the weakening of local and state party organizations, it is argued, was the devolution of power at national conventions from party leaders to candidate-centered coalitions and issue activists.

The party-decline school is noteworthy for its venerability. In their massive study of both parties' nominating processes in 1952, Paul David and his colleagues concluded that "very few of the state political conventions of 1952 were within the grip of a recognized state political boss" and that "the old-time local political bosses seem to be dying off without being replaced."[24] In 1957, in an article that should forever silence those who claim that political science cannot be predictive, William Carleton wrote:

It is probable that by 1976 or 1980 all that a nominating convention will do will be to meet to ratify the nomination for president of *the* national favorite already determined by the agencies, formal and informal, of mass democracy; to ratify the nomination for vice-president of the second leading national favorite; to endorse a platform already written by leaders responding to national and group pressures; and to stage a rally for the benefit of the national television audience. Delegates and "leaders" in national conventions, like presidential electors, will have become rubber stamps.[25]

Except for his prediction about the Vice-Presidency, perhaps overly influenced by the Kefauver experience in 1956, Carleton's prediction was on the mark. Compare his statement with that of Arthur Hadley nearly twenty years later:

Conventions have become largely ceremony and TV entertainment, their principal political function the selection of the Vice-President and a demonstration of party unity for television. Almost, but as yet not quite, the convention has gone the way of the presidential Electors.[26]

More important for our purposes, Hadley shares Carleton's view that the change in nominations was a long-term process that began to crystallize in the 1960s.[27] Another early trend-spotter was journalist Theodore White, who wrote in 1961 that partly because "the ever-greater citizen participation in politics produces more and more citizen delegates and fewer and fewer of the sheeplike masses herded at will by delegate bosses . . . conventions are now less bluntly controlled by bosses, and more sharply controlled by techniques and forces set in motion outside the convention city itself."[28] Others who emphasize long-term developments more than the effects of the rules include David Adamany, John Aldrich, Kenneth Bode and Carol Casey, Donald Fraser, Xandra Kayden, Everett Ladd and Charles Hadley, Robert Shogan, and Richard Watson.[29]

It is difficult to classify Austin Ranney. I have assigned him to the 1972 school, although in other writings Ranney has argued that the rules were not necessarily the most important cause of change and that Barry Goldwater, in prereform days, was nominated with a campaign as ideological as George McGovern's in the postreform days.[30] Since he penned those words earlier than his other assertions quoted earlier, I am using his more recent remarks as the basis for classification.

The party-decline school is apparently guided by the model of causation shown in Figure 1.2. The most important causal relationships are depicted by solid arrows, the less important by dotted arrows. Surely some members of the party-decline school would

FIGURE 1.2. Causal model of the party-decline school

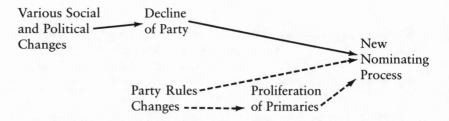

further draw an arrow indicating that the decline of party *caused* the reforms, an argument to which I shall return.

The 1936 School

A few authors date the modern era from 1936, and they will be designated the 1936 school. William Keech and Donald Matthews have been most articulate in propounding the thesis that 1936 marked a watershed because in that year came the first widespread use of public opinion surveys in reporting the Presidential campaign, and the Democrats' abolition of the two-thirds rule.[31] Gerald Pomper seems to agree with them, for he has called 1932 "the last year before the modern period of presidential races."[32] None of these authors denies that changes since 1936 have been important, but all seem to regard that year as the turning point, when the trend toward devolution of the nominating process got under way. Studies specifically devoted to the effects of the polls must necessarily begin no earlier than 1936, and so in order to determine whether the authors of such studies belong to the 1936 school we must see whether they pay attention to more recent developments. James Beniger does not, so he belongs to the 1936 school.[33] William Lucy considers the 1972 reforms significant, but with enough ambivalence that it is unclear whether he belongs to the 1972 school, if any.[34]

This causal model can be expressed as in Figure 1.3. Again, dotted-arrow relationship is less important than solid-arrow ones.

Authors differ as to what the "new nominating process" involves. Pomper emphasizes the loss of control by party leaders which I have associated with both the 1972 and the party-decline schools. Keech, Matthews, and Beniger do not seem to address this

FIGURE 1.3. Causal model of the 1936 school

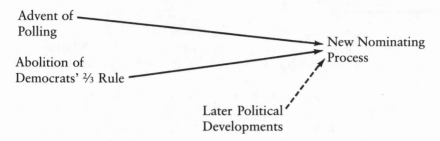

issue and may be most appropriately associated with the last school, to be discussed below. But all of them seem to agree that the 1930s, and not (as the previously discussed schools argued) later decades, produced our current nominating system.

The Stasis School

Finally we have the null hypothesis: nothing has changed. While nobody has explicitly argued this position (perhaps because, as I shall demonstrate, it is indefensible), some have implicitly done so simply by discussing national conventions as though they were still being conducted the way they were many years ago—delegation leaders have great autonomy, there is great uncertainty about the outcome of the Presidential nominating process, the result is a process of bargaining for the nomination, and conventions can last for more than one nominating ballot and even become deadlocked.

Prominent in this school are authors of rational-actor models of convention decision-making who utilize game theory—Steven Brams, Eugene McGregor, Philip Straffin, and James Zais and John Kessel.[35] These authors write as though conventions still afford delegates opportunities to jump on or off bandwagons. Eschewing mathematical formulations, Judith Parris similarly argues that conventions are still bargaining arenas.[36] Even Nelson Polsby and Aaron Wildavsky, so sensitive to the rise of ideological "purists," discuss the balloting as though uncertainty still reigned.[37]

Like any null hypothesis, this one has no causal scheme underlying it (unless one wanted to argue *why* the process remains unchanged), nor do I have to test it explicitly. If tests of the earlier-stated hypotheses indicate that nothing has changed, the stasis school will be vindicated.

The Argument of This Book

It is important to test these hypotheses, not only to understand the nature of such an important phenomenon as the Presidential nominating process but also to determine whether any changes that have occurred are due to specific reforms, *and hence reversible*, or are the product of long-term social developments that are hardly reversible at all by human will.

Now that I have presented the four schools, pigeon-holing various authors as best I could, it is time to present the hypothesis that I believe best explains most of the features of the present system— the party-decline thesis. Briefly, the hypothesis underlying this book is that *the nominating process has evolved since the early 1950s gradually into one in which state and local party leaders can no longer control nominations, and this is due to the long-term decay of party organization in the United States.* While no single hypothesis that attempts to explain so complex a set of phenomena can explain all of it, I believe and shall demonstrate that this one comes closer than any other.

I am not arguing that the rules changes have had no effect. In fact, I shall show precisely what effects they have had. In the very short run, the rules can favor one candidate over another and even decide close contests, as several authors have clearly pointed out.[38] From the perspective of party development, however, these influences can be seen to have been of fleeting significance, *unless* it can be shown that a certain *type* of candidate is *systematically* benefited, a topic to which I shall return in Chapter 6. The rules have had other kinds of consequences as well. Nevertheless, the transition to the new system was well under way by the time the McGovern-Fraser Commission held its first meeting, and most of the reforms had the ultimate effect of codifying a trend that was already developing.

Indeed, if the data substantiate my hypothesis convincingly, the reader might conclude that the 1972 school had the causal relationship exactly reversed. Instead of the reforms leading to party decline, party decline may have resulted in a vacuum left by the weakening of the old party leaders, and a new set of rules may have been necessary to routinize and legitimize what was already occurring. I shall attempt to be rigorously empirical here, and since this is a proposition that would be difficult to sustain with empirical evidence, I shall simply leave it for speculation in Chapter 8.

In some ways, both the 1972 and the party-decline schools may be right, in the way that Kirkpatrick noted: the reforms may have accelerated and reinforced the process of change. Presumably this would be yet another hypothesis that can be tested with empirical evidence.

Testing Hypotheses

Perhaps because this subject is so laden with heartfelt normative concerns, usually careful scholars sometimes misuse, or fail to use, empirical evidence in discussing these matters. The following is a brief catalog of some of these errors, presented so that my own methodology will be contrasted with these lapses.

Floating Comparisons

Assertions are sometimes made to establish that change has occurred, and they are "supported" by presentations of recent data without resorting to earlier data by way of comparison. This brings to mind the old Madison Avenue technique of claiming that a product is "90 percent better" without filling in the comparison.

Jeane Kirkpatrick is a particularly notable offender here. Her massive and enormously useful study of the 1972 national convention delegates states as its "principal hypothesis":

There were among the delegates to the two conventions of 1972 political types whose personal and political goals, resources, and styles differed in identifiable ways from those of the political actors who have dominated presidential politics in the past decades.[39]

This assertion that the 1972 delegates differed from those of the past presumably requires Kirkpatrick to compare these delegates with those attending prior conventions, but nowhere in her massive book is there such a systematic comparison. None of the tables includes data from earlier years, even when she cites the findings of Herbert McClosky and others about the differences between the opinions of delegates and their fellow partisans; it would have been enlightening to learn whether the differences she found in 1972 were greater than, less than, or equal to those McClosky found in 1956.[40] Kirkpatrick acknowledges this problem as "an obvious handicap, but . . . not ultimately disabling."[41] She makes a vague reference to earlier studies but makes no explicit use of them. Moreover, she writes,

It did not require a survey of the delegates to the 1960 and 1964 Republican conventions to establish that some significant changes had occurred, nor a survey of delegates to the 1964, 1968, and 1972 Democratic conventions to confirm that significant change was in progress.[42]

But why should we assume that just because the *outcomes* of those conventions were different, the *delegates* were different along the many dimensions Kirkpatrick studies? If we can draw such sweeping inferences, why was her exhaustive study necessary in the first place?

Nelson Polsby falls victim to this fallacy as well, attributing the recent string of first-ballot victories to "the transformation of 1968–72" without checking to see whether earlier conventions also ended on the first ballot. Polsby also sees significance in the Democrats' loss of two out of the first three postreform Presidential elections, without noting that they also lost two of the four most proximate prereform elections. Moreover, his argument that Presidential behavior has been affected by the rules is substantiated by detailed review of the performance of only one President, Jimmy Carter.[43]

On the other side of the ideological divide, Christopher Arterton cites "research conducted during the past two [1972 and 1976] Democratic conventions" to argue that the new rules undercut the role of state party leaders.[44] How can we be sure it was the rules that caused this development if he does not cite studies of the 1968 convention and earlier conventions?

Unsubstantiated Assertions

One common reference made by some critics of George McGovern's Presidential campaign was to the alleged elitism of his delegates. Judith Center calls them "well educated, relatively affluent," and Penn Kemble and Josh Muravchik suggest that the 1972 delegates may have been wealthier than those of 1968.[45] None of these authors offers empirical evidence, nor did any refrain from making such allegations before such data were available. In fact, as Kirkpatrick shows, the McGovern delegates earned *lower* incomes than did the delegates supporting his opponents, although they were more highly educated.[46] The comparison of 1972 delegates with 1968 delegates must be tempered because delegates' economic positions should be compared with the economic status of the American people and particularly the rank and file of Democrats. According to the University of Michigan Center for Political Studies surveys, the median income of Democrats in 1968 was about $6,900 and in 1972 about $8,300—a 20 percent increase. The median income of Democratic *delegates* was about $17,900 in 1968 and $20,800 in 1972—a 16 percent increase.[47] Compared with the party masses, then, the 1972 delegates' income was more representative than the 1968 delegates' income.

Other authors have similarly failed to consult relevant data that would have overturned their assertions. A good example, again from an ideological viewpoint different from that previously cited, is William Crotty's statement that the South lost power in the Democratic party as a result of the 1972 reforms.[48] While Crotty does not precisely define what the South is, I shall use the eleven former Confederate states and ascertain whether 1972 marked a drop in that region's "power." Without getting into the murky question of what power is, I shall use two quantifiable and plausible measures: proportion of the votes, and support for the winner.

The analysis begins in 1948, the year that the North-South split in the party crystallized. In Table 1.2 the proportion of convention votes held by the South from 1948 through 1984 is presented. From 1956 through 1976 there was a monotonic trend reducing Southern strength at the convention, due primarily to the South's lack of support for the national ticket in November. But notice that, whether measured in absolute terms or by percentages, the declines in 1972 and 1976 were less than those in most previous years. And in 1980 and 1984 there was a rise in Southern strength.

Table 1.3 shows Southern and non-Southern support for the Presidential nominee on key votes at all contested conventions since 1948.[49] The South failed to back the winner at every convention through 1960, gave Humphrey disproportionate support in 1968, opposed McGovern in 1972, and gave favorite son Carter a high level of support in 1976 and 1980. In 1984 the South was

TABLE 1.2. Representation of the South at Democratic national conventions, 1948–1984

Year	Percentage of votes	Absolute change	Percentage change
1948	24.1		
1952	23.6	−0.5	− 2.1
1956	24.3	+0.7	+ 3.0
1960	23.1	−1.2	− 4.9
1964	22.5	−0.6	− 2.6
1968	20.1	−2.4	−10.7
1972	19.7	−0.4	− 2.0
1976	19.2	−0.5	− 2.5
1980	21.0	+1.8	+9.4
1984	23.7	+2.7	+12.9

TABLE 1.3. Support for nominee by the South and non-South in contested Democratic national conventions, 1948–1984

Year	Nominee	Percentage of Southern vote for nominee	Percentage of non-Southern vote for nominee
1948	Truman	4.4	97.5
1952	Stevenson[a]	3.1	33.6
1956	Stevenson	47.6	71.9
1960	Kennedy	2.7	68.1
1968	Humphrey	83.5	63.0
1972	McGovern	23.6	65.6
1976	Carter	89.3	70.9
1980	Carter	86.7	57.6
1984	Mondale	53.6	56.4

[a]Second ballot; all other nominees' votes on first ballot.

only slightly less supportive of Mondale than the rest of the nation, and far less supportive of his chief rival, Gary Hart. Certainly the reforms were not associated with Southern losses, and in light of Crotty's allegation it is ironic that the nation's first nominee in 128 years to hail from the Deep South won his victory four years after the McGovern-Fraser reforms went into effect.

I have singled out these authors not because they are unusually sloppy but because their assumptions are relatively easy to test. Too much mythology has developed around these matters, and political scientists have a special responsibility not to add to the loose talk.

Incomplete Data

At times, data are used selectively or incompletely, and I shall present two examples. Stephen Hess notes that since the Democrats abolished their two-thirds rule in 1936, "only one Democratic convention (1952) has failed to make a nomination on the first ballot—proof that rules do affect outcomes."[50] Here Hess is implying that majority-vote conventions usually produce first-ballot victories, an allegation belied by the fact that twelve of the twenty-nine Whig and Republican (majority-vote) conventions from 1831 through 1952 were multiballoted. This becomes even more striking when we consider that twelve of the seventeen single-ballot conventions nominated incumbents. Had Roosevelt not sought third and fourth terms, we might have seen several multiballot Democratic conventions in this period (the Republicans had two). Indeed, this example shows how interparty comparisons can be used to test assertions that look more valid than they should when applied to only one party. In this way we can use to scholarly advantage the fact that reforms have come to each party at different times and in different ways.

Austin Ranney misleadingly presents data on the rise of independents in recent years: "When people were asked in 1964 what party they preferred, only 23 percent classed themselves as Independents; but in 1972 the proportion rose sharply to 36 percent."[51] This implication that it was not until 1972 that the proportion of independents began to rise is important because it appears to support Ranney's general thesis that 1972 was a turning point. But the data on which Ranney relies also show that this was a gradual process;

the largest increase in independents occurred from 1964 to 1966, or if only Presidential election years are considered, from 1964 to 1968.[52] Ranney's statement is misleading.

Methodology

Learning from these errors, I shall attempt to follow several important rules when testing the hypotheses discussed above: to compare recent data with earlier data whenever possible, to corroborate assertions with data, and to use data completely, without omitting important pieces of evidence or interparty comparisons. Since I do have a point of view here, the reader should hold this study to the high standard I have set for myself.

The most elegant test of the party decline hypothesis would be to establish an empirical measure of the institutional strength or weakness of state and local party organizations and then to attempt to correlate the decline in strength of each state party with changes in that state's behavior at national conventions. I do not know of any such measure, so the party decline thesis must be tested indirectly with the assumption that the decline was well under way in most states by the 1960s. This is an assumption that the party decline school makes, and it makes empirical testing convenient because it enables us to make several decision rules after observing the data:

1. If the data show no apparent trend, the stasis school seems to be vindicated.
2. If there is a sharp change in the data in 1936 and none thereafter, the 1936 school seems to be vindicated.
3. If there is a gradual change in the data that becomes particularly apparent in the 1950s and 1960s, the party-decline school seems to be vindicated.
4. If there is no change until 1972, and then there is a sharp change, the 1972 school seems to be vindicated.
5. If change began in the 1950s and 1960s and then increased in 1972, we can infer that the 1972 reforms probably accelerated a trend that was under way as a result of factors explained by the party-decline school.

Of course, the party-decline school might be credited with more than it deserves. If other factors not relevant to party decline caused changes in the nominating process in the 1950s and 1960s, we will be inferring that party decline caused them (unless the observed changes in the process seem inconsistent with the phenomenon of party decline). I know of no alternate theory that postulates that whatever changes occurred in the 1950s and 1960s were not caused by factors relevant to party decline, and until such a theory appears I shall infer that all pre-1972 changes under decision rules 3 and 5 were caused by party decline.

In the final analysis, I am always subject to the criticism that I am not using genuine controls. A sudden change in a variable from 1968 to 1972, even if it persists at the new level into 1976 and beyond, might not be due to rules changes. Perhaps that variable would have changed anyway, whether or not new rules were adopted. Without "scientific" but unachievable controls—that is, without being able to experience the post-1968 years without the McGovern-Fraser Commission—we can never know for sure. All we can do is use logic, common sense, and plausibleness. If there was such a change in a variable, and if the change seems consonant with particular rules changes, then I shall infer that the new rules were the cause. I have already done so, by explaining Table 1.1, which showed the proliferation of primaries, by the McGovern-Fraser rules.

At what time period shall we look? In order to do justice to the 1936 school, we should begin whenever possible with a year preceding that era, and it seems appropriate to go back to the critical era of the 1890s to obtain historical perspective. Not only is that period appropriate for such distancing, demarcating the beginning of the "party system" that culminated in the realignment of the 1930s,[53] but it also marked the beginning of the modern era of incumbent nominations. Chester Arthur in 1884 was the most recent President to be denied his party's nomination at the convention.

Any student of nominating conventions knows that there is a big difference between those that involve a consensus about the nominee and those that do not. It will often be appropriate to separate them, and so an operational definition of a contested convention is in order. I shall define a contested convention as one in which more than one candidate received at least 10 percent of the vote.[54] Logic cries out for one exception to this rule: at the 1912 Republican convention, William H. Taft was the only candidate to exceed 10 percent, receiving 51.6 percent. Theodore Roosevelt came in second, garnering 9.9 percent, but nearly a third of the delegates abstained. I therefore consider this a contested convention, because the vote of even one of the 348 abstainers would have put Roosevelt over the 10 percent mark.

Any arbitrary standard is open to challenge. Why call the 1976 Democratic convention contested when there was no question who the nominee would be? Had Morris Udall not insisted on being placed in nomination, as a gesture to his supporters, I would probably not be calling that a contested convention. On the other hand, the 1980 Republican convention only appears to be uncontested because all Ronald Reagan's foes withdrew by the time the roll-call vote was taken. Moreover, any cutoff will have its near misses: Jerry Brown in 1976 received 300.5 out of 3,008 votes, a fraction under 10 percent, and so he is (perhaps unfairly) not considered in the same class as Jimmy Carter and Udall. My response to all these charges is that the only way I can be objective is to set an arbitrary standard, hoping that all can agree that the standard is reasonable in principle, and that the taxonomy derived from the standard is in general also reasonable. Otherwise, I leave myself open to the charge of preselecting my cases carefully to prove my hypotheses, the most damaging charge of all.

At contested conventions, then, there are *major candidates*, those who received at least 10 percent of the vote on any ballot, and *minor candidates* or *favorite sons*, those who did not. At times it will be necessary to single out a *key vote* from each convention, and I have developed several decision rules for doing so. Their enumeration will come in Chapter 5, when they will be utilized.

One final methodological note is in order. Unlike electoral behavior or the legislative process, the nominating process is a phenomenon with a pitifully small number of cases. There have been only forty-six major-party nominations since 1896, and only fourteen since 1960; of these, only twenty-four since 1896 were contested, and only nine since 1960. A great sweep of time produces very few Ns. As of this writing, the Democrats have nominated only four candidates since the McGovern-Fraser reforms were adopted, and each party has nominated only three since the 1974 FECA amendments were passed. This makes generalizations depend on an excruciatingly small data base, and it is a problem I can only acknowledge, while hoping for the best. Because two of the hypotheses I am testing single out specific years, I shall normally not aggregate data into time periods, but present each year separately so that the reader may judge whether my inferences are appropriate. This will necessitate longer and more cumbersome tables, but I see no alternative.

In the next several chapters, I shall be looking at a number of measurable aspects of the nominating process and analyzing them in light of the hypotheses enumerated above. I have grouped the aspects to be examined thematically, and I shall conclude each chapter with a review of the aspects of nominating politics that are confirmed by each of the models I have presented. The themes to be covered are, respectively, general nominating patterns, who controls nominations, characteristics of the delegates, factions within the parties, who is nominated, and the effects of the process on our parties and the Presidency. The concluding chapter will consider the implications of these findings for reform and the real role played by the changes in the rules.

TWO

Nominating Patterns

In the heyday of boss control over nominating conventions, most observers of the process agree, party leaders had a number of resources at their disposal.[1] In order to understand how the local boss functioned, it is necessary to understand his goal, which was primarily to nominate a candidate who would be an asset to the ticket and who would cooperate with the boss on patronage. This made it necessary to establish a good relationship with the candidate who would be the nominee, preferably by making the candidate beholden to the boss by providing delegate votes at a critical moment. That moment might be early in the campaign (e.g., the legendary "For Roosevelt Before Chicago" group of 1932) or at the convention climax (e.g., the famous Vice-Presidential "deal" between Roosevelt and Garner that year).

Given such goals, it was in the interest of the party leaders to maintain maximum flexibility so that if an unforeseen nominee began to emerge at the convention, a savvy boss could jump on his bandwagon at a strategic juncture. This meant that in the absence of a consensual nominee, who by definition would not find it necessary to bargain with anyone, the nomination should be kept from the winner as long as possible. Moreover, it meant that each boss's delegation should refrain from committing itself too early and too strongly to a candidate, so that its votes would be available for horse-trading by the leader. These considerations resulted in a number of convention features familiar to students of political lore. One was the large number of uncommitted delegates, whom the bosses could use as bargaining chips. A variation of this was the favorite son candidacy, a convenient way to keep one's delegates from other candidates until the bargaining began while also giving

24

recognition to a local hero who might even, with some luck, end up as the nominee. Another feature of the older conventions was the length of the nominating process, which could be considerable if enough leaders held onto their delegates waiting for the best bargaining opportunity. This meant several or even dozens of ballots, with numerous candidates placed in nomination. It also encouraged late entries and the emergence of legendary dark horses, the James K. Polks and Warren G. Hardings. And the atmosphere of uncertainty put a special premium on prenominating roll-call ballots to test the strength of the leading candidates and provide clues about who might win.

None of the four schools described in Chapter 1 denies that conventions used to take that form. The issues are whether nominations are still decided that way, and if not, why not. In this chapter I shall consider in turn each of the convention features noted above.

The Decline of the Uncommitted

Two Democratic activists, each representing a different portion of the ideological spectrum, have asserted that the new rules tend to decrease the proportion of uncommitted delegates. Rick Stearns, of the 1972 McGovern campaign, argued that the McGovern-Fraser rule requiring that delegates running in primaries indicate their Presidential preferences had the effect of diminishing the uncommitted bloc.[2] Antireform leader Penn Kemble subsequently maintained that the proportional representation rules would have the same effect.[3] Nelson Polsby has argued that in general primary electorates prefer not to vote for uncommitted delegates.[4] But Denis Sullivan and his colleagues argued the party-decline thesis: that a number of trends since 1945, including the rules, resulted in fewer uncommitteds.[5]

Who is right? I have compiled journalists' delegate counts from the weekends before each contested convention since 1952, except for the cut-and-dried Democratic convention of 1976, when the media did not bother to count after Carter secured the nomination in early June. I could not find any precise counts from before 1952. Table 2.1 shows a monotonic drop among Democratic uncommitteds from 1952 through 1980, with the greatest decline occurring

TABLE 2.1. Percentage of delegates uncommitted the weekend before each contested convention, 1952–1984

Year	Percentage	Source
A. Democrats		
1952	29.3	*New York Times*, July 20, 1952, sec. 1, p. 34
1956	27.8	*New York Times*, August 13, 1956, p. 13
1960	24.2	*Washington Post*, July 10, 1960, p. A6
1968	11.9	*New York Times*, August 25, 1968, sec. 1, p. 1
1972	7.3	*Washington Post*, July 9, 1972, p. A2
1976	—[a]	
1980	3.1	*Washington Post*, August 10, 1980, p. C5
B. Republicans		
1952	9.8	*New York Times*, July 6, 1952, sec. 1, p. 36
1964	15.4	*New York Times*, July 12, 1964, sec. 1, p. 57
1968	3.8	*New York Times*, August 4, 1968, sec. 1, p. 1
1976	4.7	*New York Times*, August 15, 1976, sec. 1, p. 24

[a]No count available, as nomination was not in doubt.

not in 1972 or 1976 but in 1968. It is likely that had Robert Kennedy not been assassinated the figure for 1968 would have been still lower. Similarly, the chief Republican drop occurred between 1964 and 1968. Of course, these data are dependent on many factors, notably the number of serious candidates left by the time of the convention and how far ahead the front-runner is, but clearly the rules did not cause a major decline in the uncommitted bloc, and equally clearly, the decline in uncommitteds was occurring before 1972.

Fewer Favorite Sons

The Commission on Rules, or O'Hara Commission, one of the reform commissions established in the wake of the 1968 Democratic convention, stipulated that nominating speeches could be made only for candidates who could secure at least fifty delegate signatures.[6] Because twenty delegations to the party's 1972 convention had at least fifty votes, this was not a draconian rule, but a proponent of the 1972 model could argue that it might have undercut favorite son candidacies. Another rule that might have had the same effect was the rule cited by Rick Stearns above, that would-be delegates express a Presidential preference in the primaries. Primary voters might be unwilling to vote for a delegate whose preference was not for a major candidate. Indeed, this was also Nelson Polsby's argument, cited above.

Has there been a decline in favorite sons, and if so, when did it begin? Table 2.2 shows for each contested convention since 1896 the proportion of first-ballot votes that were won by minor candidates (those receiving less than 10 percent). The Democrats' 1936 rules change seems to have had an impact, for shortening the balloting probably discouraged long-shot candidacies. After 1960, however, there was a further drop-off. The 1896–1932 mean was 28.9, the 1948–1960 mean was 15.1, and the 1968–1984 mean was 7.4. Without a rules change in 1936, the Republicans have also had a clear and almost monotonic drop-off since the zenith in 1916. The post-1948 conventions are clearly different from earlier ones. Here again the party decline hypothesis is most convincing, with 1936 apparently important for the Democrats.

Number of Ballots

It has been decades since either party has taken more than one ballot to nominate a President. The most recent Republican multi-ballot convention was in 1948, and Democrats held theirs in 1952. As many have pointed out, this means that conventions no longer decide nominations; instead, the nominee arrives at the convention with enough delegates to secure a victory. In the words of Max

TABLE 2.2. Percentage of votes on first ballots of contested conventions going to candidates who individually received less than 10 percent of the vote, 1896–1984

Year	Democratic	Republican
1896	49.6	—
1904	14.2	—
1912	5.9	6.2 [a]
1916	—	53.2
1920	40.2	35.7
1924	38.8	—
1932	24.8	—
1940	—	34.6
1948	3.4	25.5
1952	18.3	9.2
1956	18.7	—
1960	20.1	—
1964	—	16.1
1968	10.0	13.7
1972	12.6	—
1976	11.9	0.1
1980	1.7	—
1984	0.7	—

[a] Not including vote for Theodore Roosevelt or abstentions.

Frankel, the delegates "come to the convention simply to be unwrapped and counted."[7] Or, as a Republican politician said in 1980, "You could have these conventions by mail."[8]

Indeed, every contested convention since 1952 has been a game of "try to stop the front-runner," and the front-runner has won every time. Other candidates have resorted to platform fights (the Republicans in 1964), credentials challenges (the Democrats in 1972), and rules battles (the Republicans in 1976 and the Democrats in 1980), but all to no avail. Skeptics will say that Kennedy could have been stopped in 1960 (he had only 45 votes more than a majority), Nixon in 1968 (25 votes), McGovern in 1972 (109.28

votes on the crucial California credentials vote), and Ford in 1976 (57 votes). But clearly there is a bandwagon effect, and as the old saw has it, there are always enough delegates with aspirations for a U.S. attorneyship to put any candidate with close to 50 percent over the top.

Nelson Polsby has implied that this trend dates from "the transformation of 1968–72,"[9] but if anything the trend seems to confirm the thesis of the party-decline school. There was a long-term decline in the frequency of multiballot conventions until they disappeared in the 1950s. The Democrats had labored under the notorious two-thirds rule until 1936, so the Republicans will provide the most useful longitudinal data, uninterrupted by relevant rules changes. Because of the well-known ability of incumbents to win nomination on the first ballot, I am presenting only data from conventions that did not nominate incumbents, divided by partisan eras. In the 1856–1892 period, five of the seven such Republican conventions were multiballot (71 percent); from 1896 through 1924, two out of four (50 percent); and from 1928 through 1948, two out of five (40 percent). Here is a good example of the problem of small Ns mentioned in Chapter 1. Nevertheless, the trend is in the direction predicted by the party-decline school. This is especially so when we add the years from 1952 to 1984, when none of the five such conventions lasted longer than one ballot.

Some have predicted that the post-1968 rules changes would result in more multiballot conventions—Ohio's former Governor John Gilligan, William Keech and Donald Matthews, Jeane Kirkpatrick, Judith Parris, and Nelson Polsby and Aaron Wildavsky.[10] This is a plausible argument, for it is based on the expectation that proportional representation, as mandated by the Mikulski Commission, would enable so many candidates to win delegates in so many states that nobody would be able to win a majority of convention delegates. Moreover, the matching fund and spending ceiling provisions of the 1974 FECA amendments would seem to encourage the participation of more candidates than ever, thereby dividing the pie further.

There are problems in testing the hypothesis that there are more candidates entering the race today than before. For one thing, many a candidate in the past waited in the wings, hoping to be regarded as a latter-day Cincinnatus and be plucked from his plow. Conversely, there are literally hundreds of announced candidates, especially now that the Federal Election Commission requires a statement of candidacy before one can collect contributions. Even when a recognized political figure announces, how serious is his (Milton Shapp's) or her (Shirley Chisholm's) candidacy?[11]

But we *can* say that all the conventions under these new rules were decided in one ballot. The prediction might still be borne out in the future, but it clearly has not been an immediate consequence of the rules. Why not? Paul David and James Ceaser suggest that proportional representation may aid prominent candidates by guaranteeing them a large bloc of delegates.[12] This was not borne out by the results of the open contests of 1976, 1980, and 1984, when such lesser-known candidates as Jimmy Carter, Morris Udall, George Bush, John Anderson, and Gary Hart outpolled such big names as George Wallace, Birch Bayh, John Connally, Howard Baker, and John Glenn. I suspect that the one-ballot convention has survived because the costs of campaigning have had the effect of destroying the candidacies of anyone who did not accumulate an early share of delegates. A Bayh or a Baker might hope to hobble to the convention with a potentially critical 10 percent of the vote, but the cost of getting through the primaries on a shrinking base of contributions is prohibitive. This is another hypothesis that does not lend itself conveniently to empirical analysis, although if it is true it may be one of the most significant effects of the proliferation of primaries. In short, campaign costs, despite the equalizing effects of the FECA, override the fragmentizing effects of proportional representation to guarantee more single-ballot conventions.

Proliferation of Candidates

Despite these reservations about our ability to test empirically the proposition that more candidates are participating in the race, those who argue that the rules encourage such participation deserve more of a hearing.[13] If more candidates are indeed entering the race, then even though conventions are still being decided on the first ballot more candidates should be sharing the vote.

How can we determine whether a greater number of serious candidates are entering the fray? In other words, how can we factor out those candidates who receive only a trace of the vote? A cutoff of 1 percent seems to divide the favorite sons and daughters from the idiosyncratic candidates who are backed by only a handful of delegates. Has the number of candidates who received at least 1 percent of the vote at contested conventions increased in recent years? It is important to distinguish between single-ballot and multiballot conventions here, because the latter will naturally tend to draw more candidates than the former, and the former type of convention has been the rule in recent decades. Table 2.3 displays the single-ballot, contested conventions since 1896 and how many candidates received at least 1 percent of the votes at each of them. By this measure, there has certainly been no proliferation of candidates, and perhaps even a decline.

But Table 2.3 is not an entirely satisfactory test of the proposition, given the tendency of a number of serious candidates to withdraw from the race after losing one or two primaries. Therefore, another test of whether the race has been attracting more candidates is the number of serious entrants into the primaries. Here I shall define "serious" as garnering at least 10 percent of the vote in any primary. This will count not only those whose candidacies lasted until the convention but also those who made a reasonably strong early showing but dropped out and released their delegates

TABLE 2.3. Number of candidates receiving at least 1 percent of the vote at single-ballot, contested conventions, both major parties, 1896–1984

Year	Democratic	Republican
1904	6	—
1912	—	4
1948	3	—
1952	—	4
1956	8	—
1960	8	—
1964	—	6
1968	4	9
1972	7	—
1976	3	2
1980	2	—
1984	3	—

before the convention. Unfortunately it also includes local favorite sons and daughters and stalking-horses for major candidates, and my assumption is that their inclusion will not seriously affect the long-term trend. Table 2.4 shows the results, and it is difficult to credit the rules with drawing more candidates into the contest. On the Democratic side, there was a surge from 1952 through 1976, but the number has declined since then. As for the Republicans, there appears to be little trend there, and certainly no longitudinal increase in the number of candidates.[14]

Longer Nominating Races

If party leaders no longer control the process, nominations go to those who campaign hard for them. No longer can an Adlai Ste-

TABLE 2.4. Number of candidates winning at least 10 percent of the vote in at least one primary, contested conventions, 1912–1984

Year	Democratic	Republican
1912	4	3
1916	—	12
1920	6	8
1924	5	—
1932	5	—
1940	—	7
1948	3	9
1952	10	5
1956	3	—
1960	9	—
1964	—	9
1968	8	5
1972	9	—
1976	11	2
1980	3	—
1984	5	—

venson sit back and wait for party leaders to nominate him without so much as declaring his candidacy. This seems to be reflected in the background of nominees. In Chapter 6, I shall discuss how the current nominating process is biased against candidates with jobs (besides the Presidency itself) that commit their time, such as governors and congressional leaders. Moreover, I shall demonstrate that in most recent years the poorer the attendance record in the year before the convention, the better the member of Congress did in the nomination battle.

Several authors have argued that a number of recent changes in the rules have lengthened the process—that the proliferation of primaries forces candidates to organize those states early, that proportional representation encourages them to contest many primaries, and that the Federal Election Campaign Act requires them to declare their candidacies early in order to get publicity and qualify for matching funds from the government.[15] On the contrary, argue Kenneth Bode and Carol Casey, early starts have long been an asset, as John Kennedy showed in 1960 and Richard Nixon demonstrated in 1968.[16]

It is almost impossible to measure when a campaign begins. A candidate's decision to run is usually an evolutionary process, and there is often an unofficial drive by supporters even before the decision is made. Once the die is cast, the candidate usually waits until the time seems ripe before making a formal announcement, working either quietly or not so quietly for the nomination in the meantime. The only definite moment comes when the formal announcement is made, and even that was a step often not taken by candidates in an earlier age when the myth of Cincinnatus had more potency. Indeed, my attempt to identify announcement dates for all major candidates contains numerous gaps before 1932.

Nevertheless, I shall use the formal announcement dates as an index of when a campaign begins—not because I have a great deal of confidence in these data on their face but for two pragmatic reasons. One is that I can see no alternative, and the other is that I am interested in trends over time. Even if the dates themselves are not meaningful, we should expect to see announcement dates getting earlier over time if campaigns are indeed getting longer. In other words, the announcement date is assumed to be positively correlated with the date the campaign "really" began, however the reader wishes to define it.

For each major candidate at each contested convention since 1932, I have calculated the number of days between his announcement and the opening of the convention. These are presented in Table 2.5. The data for the Democrats in 1952 and 1968 must be regarded with some caution, for in both cases an incumbent President dropped out of the race after the New Hampshire primary, encouraging other entrants (particularly those friendly to the President) to announce later than they otherwise might have.

In general, we can see longer campaigns in recent years, which seems to buttress the arguments of the 1972 school. McGovern, Ford, Carter, and Mondale established a modern record for nominees by announcing well over a year before the convention. While the 1980 Republican convention was uncontested, that year's Republican candidate announcements followed the trend. The nominee, Ronald Reagan, announced 244 days before the convention, and his two closest competitors, George Bush and John Anderson, announced respectively 440 and 402 days prior to the opening gavel. On the other hand, the data also show a gradual upward trend for nominees. Democratic nominees in 1956 and 1960 announced earlier than those of 1932 and 1944, and Republicans show an almost monotonic trend from 1940 to 1976. Complicating these trends is the fact that when *all* major candidates are observed (see the last column of Table 2.5), the Democratic trend is similar to that for nominees, but the Republican data are quite different. The 1976 Republican average is not much higher than those of the 1940s, and until 1976 there was a trend toward *shorter* campaigns.

Perhaps the most judicious conclusion to draw from these murky data is that while nominees' campaigns *have* been getting longer over the years, the rate of increase has accelerated since 1968.

The Extinct Dark Horse

Polsby and Wildavsky argue that, for reasons unspecified, the recent rules changes have prevented candidates from coming from behind to win.[17] This is a corollary of the fact that recent conventions have all been decided on the first ballot. I can only repeat my argument about that phenomenon here. It has been many years

TABLE 2.5. Number of days before the convention opened that major candidates in contested conventions formally announced their candidacies, 1932–1984

Year	Nominee	Others	Mean
A. Democrats			
1932	156	141	148.5
1948	126	0	63.0
1952	0	90, 144, 180	103.5
1956	272	91	181.5
1960	191	6	98.5
1968	121	270	195.5
1972	539	179, 234	317.3
1976	582	597	589.5
1980	251	279	265.0
1984	511	256, 515	427.3
B. Republicans			
1940	44	326, 540	303.3
1948	157	242, 552	317.0
1952	183	265	224.0
1964	192	31	111.5
1968	185	0, 97	94.0
1976	405	270	337.5

since a dark horse won, so the rules changes did not create that phenomenon. The last time a Republican front-runner was stopped was in 1940, and the last time for a Democrat was in 1952. The last nominees who started with less than 10 percent on the first ballot—true dark horses—were Warren G. Harding in 1920 and John W. Davis in 1924.

If we change the definition of dark horse to indicate someone who started out behind in the preprimary polls, Polsby and Wildavsky have an argument consistent with their first one: The reforms give the advantage to well-known politicians because financial restrictions place a special burden on obscure candidates, who have a harder time raising money.[18] To test this, I have compiled a list of the front-runners in Gallup polls at the beginning of each election year (see Table 2.6). Democratic dark horse nominations were frequent before 1972 and frequent thereafter, with about half the nominations in each period involving the overtaking of the winter front-runner. Republicans have seldom stopped the front-runner in either period. The uncontested 1980 convention fits the pattern, as Reagan was both the early front-runner and the nominee. If we use this interpretation of the meaning of dark horse, the no-change (or possibly the 1936) argument seems to hold.

Prenomination Roll-Call Votes

Has the nature of test votes that deal with rules, credentials, or the platform changed in recent years, and have the new rules affected those changes? Christopher Arterton writes:

Formerly national conventions were the highest decision-making bodies on a range of questions besides the presidential nominations. Delegates currently arrive at conventions due to their relationship to a political candidate; other matters tend to become compressed along that dimension of conflict.[19]

Arterton's assertion is in keeping with arguments that candidate organizations have become the loci of power at national conventions and that delegates are more candidate-bound than ever. The only problem is that there has been no real change in this area over the years. More than twenty years ago, Richard Bain demonstrated over many conventions the close linkage of non-nominating roll-call votes with the division on the nominating ballot(s).[20] The first question is whether the incidence of prenominating votes has increased, and this is answered in Table 2.7, which shows an increase on the Democratic side that apparently began in 1968 and a paucity of such votes on the Republican side since 1912, with no trend. If the subject matter of the Democratic votes is any indication, the increase in the incidence of such votes reflects the ideological divisions of American politics since the 1960s, including the

TABLE 2.6. Front-runners in Gallup poll, January or February of years of contested conventions, and nominees, 1940–1984

Year	Early front-runner	Nominee
A. Democrats		
1948	Harry S. Truman	Harry S. Truman
1952	Harry S. Truman (C. Estes Kefauver after Truman's withdrawal)	Adlai E. Stevenson
1956	Adlai E. Stevenson	Adlai E. Stevenson
1960	John F. Kennedy	John F. Kennedy
1968	Lyndon B. Johnson (Eugene J. McCarthy after Johnson's withdrawal)	Hubert H. Humphrey
1972	Edmund S. Muskie	George S. McGovern
1976	Edward M. Kennedy (Hubert H. Humphrey with Kennedy's name removed)	Jimmy Carter
1980	Jimmy Carter	Jimmy Carter
1984	Walter F. Mondale	Walter F. Mondale
B. Republicans		
1940	Thomas E. Dewey	Wendell L. Willkie
1948	Thomas E. Dewey	Thomas E. Dewey
1952	Dwight D. Eisenhower and Robert A. Taft (tie)	Dwight D. Eisenhower
1964	Richard M. Nixon	Barry M. Goldwater
1968	Richard M. Nixon	Richard M. Nixon
1976	Gerald R. Ford Jr.	Gerald R. Ford Jr.

Sources: *Gallup Opinion Index*, nos. 32, 125, 127, 129, 174, 175, 224.

TABLE 2.7. Number of prenomination roll-call votes, contested conventions, 1896–1984

Year	Democratic	Republican
1896	5	—
1904	1	—
1912	4	7
1916	—	0
1920	3	0
1924	3	—
1932	5	—
1940	—	0
1948	2	0
1952	2	3
1956	0	—
1960	0	—
1964	—	1
1968	7	0
1972	7	—
1976	1	1
1980	6	—
1984	4	—

Vietnam War, abortion, affirmative action, national health insurance, and nuclear weapons, as well as rules changes.

The second question is whether these votes are more likely today than in the past to be correlated with the fight for the Presidential nomination. In Table 2.8 are listed Pearson's correlation coefficients between prenominating roll-call votes and peak votes for major Presidential candidates. For each convention, I took the highest such correlation, whether it involved the nominee or not. This was on the theory that if a nominee was a compromise candidate his vote might not have reflected the main factional split at the convention. It is worth noting that all the coefficients in this table are statistically significant at the .001 level.[21] Democratic coefficients have generally been higher since 1932 than earlier, and Republican coefficients have consistently been remarkably high.

TABLE 2.8. Maximum Pearson's correlation coefficient between a
prenominating roll-call vote and the vote for a major candidate,
contested conventions, 1896–1984 (all coefficients significant at the
.001 level)

Year	Prenominating vote	Candidate	Pearson's r
A. Democrats			
1896	Financial platform plank	Patterson	.595
1904	Illinois credentials	Parker[a]	.748
1912	South Dakota credentials	Wilson[a]	.744
1920	Bryan prohibition plank	Cox[a]	.442
1924	First adjournment vote	McAdoo	.744
1932	Minnesota credentials	Roosevelt[a]	.953
1948	Moody civil rights platform plank	Truman[a]	.972
1952	Adjournment	Kefauver	.707
1968	Vietnam platform plank	Humphrey[a]	.924
1972	First California credentials vote	McGovern[a]	.858
1976	Platform	Carter[a]	.635
1980	Release delegates from pledges	Carter[a]	.909
1984	No first use of nuclear weapons	Mondale[a]	.583
B. Republicans			
1912	California credentials	W. H. Taft[a]	.989
1952	Georgia credentials	R. A. Taft	.973
1964	Civil rights platform plank	Goldwater[a]	.916
1976	Naming running-mate	Ford[a]	.942

[a] Nominee

The role of prenominating roll-call votes has not been affected by rules changes, either in their incidence or in their correlation with candidacies.

Conclusions

Nominating races are far different today from what they were at any time in the past, and this is revealed in most of the indicators used in this chapter. There are fewer uncommitted delegates as conventions open; fewer votes go to favorite sons and daughters; Presidential nominations are decided on the first ballot; and major candidates are entering the race earlier. On several measures there does not seem to have been much change over the years, including the number of candidates running, the chances of nominating the early front-runner, and the role of prenominating roll-call votes.

What caused the changes noted above? It seems apparent that the McGovern-Fraser and later rules were not responsible, for most of the changes—in uncommitted delegates, in favorite sons and daughters, and in the number of nominating ballots—clearly began before 1972. About only one development, earlier entries, can we discern a change beginning in the 1970s, and even on this measure there are signs of earlier change.

If the rules did not cause these changes, what did? The argument of the party-decline school seems to make sense here, for as state and local party leaders began to lose their grip on local political activists, they became unable to keep them from supporting major Presidential candidates. Delegates saw no advantage in being un-committed or in backing a local favorite, and their party leaders could not compel them to do so by withholding patronage or other obsolete practices. If a candidate seemed to have a real shot at the nomination, he could win delegates in droves, and one such candi-date would win enough to secure nomination on the first ballot. The old practices of party leaders—keeping their delegates away from the leading candidates, waiting for the opportune moment, bargaining, striking a deal—gradually became extinct well before the parties began to change their convention rules in any signifi-cant way.

Under these circumstances, it was to a candidate's advantage to get into the race early and win all those delegates who were up for grabs. This may be why we can see a gradual lengthening of campaigns. On the other hand, that process seems to have accelerated after 1968, and like some advocates of the 1972 school we can single out two reforms that probably had some impact on this matter. The proliferation of primaries necessitated a more public entry into the race at an earlier moment than had previously been necessary, and the 1974 FECA amendments encouraged early announcements in order to qualify for matching funds. But it is important to stress that even this trend had begun earlier.

Now that I have sketched some of the major contours of the present nominating process, I shall in the next few chapters investigate more specialized subjects: who controls nominations, who the delegates are, intraparty factionalism, who is nominated, and effects of the process on the parties and the Presidency.

THREE

Who Controls the Nominations?

The major changes in nominating patterns outlined in Chapter 4 indicate that the power centers that control conventions have changed dramatically over the years. What were those changes? In what ways have the wielders of power in previous eras gained or lost the power to control nominations? If they have lost, what new power centers have arisen? What empirical data can we examine to test these questions? First I shall discuss three prominent power centers of past conventions: state governors, party organization stalwarts, and incumbent Presidents. Then the focus will shift to two institutions given greater prominence in recent years: primaries and candidate organizations.

Gubernatorial Power

No assertion about changes in the nominating process is more central to the standard wisdom than the proposition that traditional party elites are far less influential than they were in the past. This is interpreted as a step forward by those who see the old days as dominated by corrupt and unaccountable "boss rule," and as a step backward by those who lament the destruction of the political party as an institution. Regardless of one's position on the desirability of this change, we can study whether it has occurred. There is no better place to begin than with state governors, the heads of state parties with control over state patronage, fabled in convention lore as the kingpins of nominations in the past.[1] Before 1960 they frequently were chosen as Presidential nominees (see Chapter

6), and most governors serve as delegates at most conventions (see Chapter 4). There is also much anecdotal material attesting to their role at conventions. In 1952, Robert Taft attributed his defeat at the Republican convention in part to the opposition of most Republican governors; although Taft was supported by most congressional Republicans, "the governors had far more political influence on delegates."[2] Four years later, at the 1956 Democratic convention, Senator John McClellan told Robert Kennedy: "Just get one thing through your head . . . Senators have no votes; I'm lucky to be a delegate; Orval Faubus is the governor of Arkansas, and that's it; and where he goes the Arkansas delegation goes."[3] It is worth noting that in 1956 McClellan had been a senator for thirteen years, ranked twelfth in seniority, and was a committee chairman; Faubus had been governor for less than two years.

Since then, we are told, gubernatorial power at conventions has plummeted. Donald Fraser, ordinarily a member of what I have called the party-decline school, attributed this decline and that of other high officials to the rules.[4] Nelson Polsby and Aaron Wildavsky, who blame the rules for other developments, cite a gradual decline since the 1950s and lay stress on the claim that, because fewer gubernatorial races occur in Presidential election years, governors are less interested in influencing the selection of the Presidential nominee.[5]

One relatively straightforward way to assess gubernatorial influence is to determine whom the governor endorsed and then see whether a majority of the state's delegation voted for that candidate. This required painstaking research, and there were gaps in the data. I therefore went back only to 1952, and for each contested convention I was able to identify the preferences of at least 58 percent of that party's governors (the mean was 77 percent). In some cases I was unable to identify a preference because there was none.

Table 3.1 shows how many governors with an expressed preference led delegations that shared that preference. At first blush, the 1972 school seems to provide the best interpretation of the data, for the success rates in both parties declined substantially after 1968. But the data are not easy to interpret. For one thing, candidates in recent years have had a tendency to drop out of the race before the convention, depressing the success rates of governors who endorsed them. Such dropouts included Humphrey and Mus-

TABLE 3.1. Of governors who endorsed candidates at contested major-party national conventions, the percentage whose delegations backed their favored candidates by a majority of the votes, 1952–1984 (figures in parentheses denote number of governors making endorsements)

Year	Democratic rate	Republican rate
1952	80.0	85.7
	(20)	(21)
1956	70.6	—
	(17)	
1960	85.2	—
	(27)	
1964	—	76.9
		(13)
1968	83.3	80.0
	(18)	(20)
1972	42.9	—
	(21)	
1976	33.3	53.8
	(21)	(13)
1980	63.0	—
	(27)	
1984	60.9	—
	(23)	

kie in 1972, Church, Jackson, and Wallace in 1976, and Glenn in 1984. Thirteen Democratic governors endorsed Humphrey or Muskie in 1972, eight endorsed Church, Jackson, or Wallace in 1976, and three backed Glenn in 1984. When these candidates left the race, delegates who wanted to follow their governor's lead were left stranded.

Another factor is the increasing success rate of insurgent candidates, for reasons that pervade this book. Their greater success should almost inevitably hurt the success rate of governors, who usually oppose insurgents. To determine whether this is true, it is necessary to define who is an "insurgent" candidate and who represents the "establishment." I shall designate as insurgents Mc-Govern, Wallace, and Chisholm in 1972, Carter until the primaries ended in 1976, Kennedy in 1980, and Hart and Jackson in 1984. (Carter was an insurgent at the outset of his campaign in 1976, but by the time of the convention the party establishment had swung its support to him.) A careful look at the four most recent Democratic conventions shows that where governors' plans were thwarted it was almost invariably a case of an insurgent raiding the delegation after the governor endorsed an establishment figure. The reverse seldom occurred, and so the decline in gubernatorial power is a development that is highly dependent on the circumstances of the race in that state. Governors who back insurgents usually do better than governors who back establishment candidates, and so the decline in gubernatorial power is not an across-the-board phenomenon. All four Democratic governors who backed McGovern or Wallace in 1972 were successful, but only five of the seventeen who did not were successful. Five of the six who backed Carter before June 1976 secured Carter delegations; only two of the fifteen who endorsed others were similarly successful. This comparison cannot be made for 1980, when only Governor Joseph Brennan of Maine endorsed Kennedy; and in 1968 and 1984 too few governors opposed Humphrey or Mondale, respectively, to provide a meaningful test.

The same logic can be applied to Republicans in 1964, with the assumption that Barry Goldwater was the insurgent candidate. All five Republican governors who endorsed Goldwater brought Goldwater delegations to the convention, but only five of the eight anti-Goldwater governors were successful. In 1976 there was no difference between the success rates of pro-Ford governors and pro-Reagan governors; however, only two governors backed Reagan that year, so not much should be inferred from this.

I therefore conclude that while governors do seem less successful at swinging their states to their favorite candidates, and while this change began in 1972, it is unclear whether the rules hurt them. Confounding factors include the departure from the race of gubernatorial favorites, and the rise of strong insurgent campaigns. Governors who back insurgents have not been weak in recent years, but governors who back establishment candidates are. The key factor here may be whom the governor endorsed, not gubernatorial weakness per se.

Power of Party Leaders

Do party leaders tend to get their way at conventions less often than they used to, and if so, when did the decline begin? In the preceding section, I might have measured gubernatorial influence by seeing whom the majority of governors favored and then seeing if that candidate were nominated. Because I was unable to determine the preference of every governor, it seems most prudent to mention more than one Presidential candidate if there were a small difference between the most popular and the second most popular candidates.

This approach can be applied to other party elites, especially those for whom data on the preferences of individuals are unavailable. From 1952 until 1972 the Gallup surveyers also questioned county chairpersons of both parties as to their preferences, and the results give us another group of often powerful party officials to examine.[6] For 1976 and 1980, I shall investigate polls of national and state committee leaders conducted by *U.S. News & World Report*, and for 1984 a similar poll, conducted by *Newsweek*, will be used.[7] Finally, I shall compare the preferences of these leaders with the outcome of the primaries. This can be done in two ways: by seeing who won the most primaries and by seeing who won the most votes in all the primaries combined. The first measure is highly dependent on how many primaries, and where, each candidate entered; the second is affected by these factors as well as by the number of voters participating in each primary and the nationwide distribution of participation. For example, if the turnout rate in the California primary is high, a candidate might win only that primary and amass more votes than any other candidate. Unless otherwise noted, the same candidate won both the most primaries and the most votes.

Table 3.2 shows whether organizational leaders had their way more than primary voters did and any changes that might have occurred over time. Both the 1972 and the party-decline schools would expect that organizational leaders' preferences would dominate in the earlier years and primary voters' wishes in later years. The 1972 school, however, would anticipate an abrupt change beginning in 1972, while the party-decline school would expect a much more gradual transition. The results on the Democratic side seem to confirm the 1972 school's argument, because organizational leaders did not clearly back the loser until 1972 and 1976, while the last time the clear-cut winner of the primaries lost a Democratic nomination was in 1968. This is in keeping with the effect of the proliferation of primaries, to be discussed below. On the other hand, note that governors chose wrong only once, in 1972.

On the Republican side the situation is different. The data for 1952 show that *only* the Republican governors backed the winner, and in 1964 *only* the same group backed the losers. In recent years, both leaders and "followers" backed the winning candidate. I should add that in 1980, members of the Republican national and state committees expressed a preference for George Bush although most Republican governors and voters backed Ronald Reagan.[8] Here there is no clear trend, and if anything the leaders are getting better at choosing winners. One might argue that the rules did make the difference here, affecting the Democrats more than the Republicans. The problem is to explain why the rules should have affected one party more than the other, especially when the change that was most likely to have been responsible—the proliferation of primaries—affected both parties equally.

If Republican leaders are getting better at picking the winners, is it because they are really expressing an independent a priori judgment, or do they wait to see who is ahead and then jump on the bandwagon? I tried to factor out such bandwagon-jumpers among the Democrats in 1976 by ignoring endorsements after the beginning of June, when Carter secured the nomination. But this is a phenomenon that can never be precisely measured. It suggests that Democratic leaders might be getting less proficient, and Republican leaders more proficient, at spotting winners early. (This may be because in recent years Republicans have been more prone than Democrats to nominate the early front-runner in the Gallup poll [see Table 2.6]). The trends in Table 3.2 may say less about the *power* of leaders than about their ability to handicap the race.

Incumbency

Surely no party leader is more prominent than the President of the United States, especially when he is a candidate for another term.[9] Yet the question of whether Presidential incumbents have a

TABLE 3.2. Nomination preferences of various groups of partisans, contested conventions, 1952–1984

Year	Governors[a]	Organization[b]	Primaries	Nominee
A. Democrats				
1952	Stevenson Russell	Stevenson	Kefauver	Stevenson
1956	Stevenson	Stevenson	Stevenson[c] Kefauver[d]	Stevenson
1960	Kennedy	Kennedy	Kennedy	Kennedy
1968	Humphrey	Humphrey	McCarthy	Humphrey
1972	Muskie	Humphrey	Humphrey[c] McGovern[d]	McGovern
1976	Carter Jackson	Humphrey	Carter	Carter
1980	Carter	Carter	Carter	Carter
1984	Mondale	Mondale	Mondale[c] Hart[d]	Mondale
B. Republicans				
1952	Eisenhower	Taft	Taft	Eisenhower
1964	Rockefeller Scranton	Goldwater	Goldwater	Goldwater
1968	Nixon Rockefeller	Nixon	Nixon	Nixon
1976	Ford	Ford	Ford	Ford

[a] If two names, first two choices were nearly equal in degree of support.

[b] 1952–1972, Gallup survey of county chairpersons (see note 6). 1976–1984, *U.S. News* and *Newsweek* polls of national and state committee members and other party notables (see note 7).

[c] Winner of the most primary votes.

[d] Winner of the most primaries.

hard or easy time of winning nomination is one of the most complex. On the one hand, no incumbent since 1884 has made an effort at the convention and lost.[10] On the other hand, Johnson was driven from the race in 1968, and Ford and Carter had to wage hard fights to win their nominations in 1976 and 1980.[11] Therefore we have to explain a trend, and also identify what it is.

There are great resources available to an incumbent, resources only too painfully evident to Reagan in 1976 and Kennedy in 1980.[12] Besides such factors as the ability to capture the attention of the mass media and power over many federal grants, the President is said to be helped or harmed by changing party rules. Reagan's 1976 manager, John Sears, later attributed much of Ford's advantage to the proliferation of primaries and the FECA spending limitations, which combined to restrict Reagan severely.[13] A Ford adviser, Robert Teeter, responded that Ford was hurt by spending limits too, but he conceded the Presidential advantage in such matters as press coverage and the White House staff.[14] On the other hand, Edward Banfield argues that incumbents are hurt by their need to appeal to voters in the primaries and can expect to lose at least as often as they win.[15]

This puts us in something of a social science quandary, for when such a diversity of empirical observations and explanations exists, it is possible to argue for any theory. If incumbents are better off than they used to be, Sears can blame some of the rules; if incumbents are worse off, Teeter and Banfield can blame other rules; and if there has been no change, perhaps different rules canceled each other out. In an attempt to sort out the problem, I shall first resort to the quantitative evidence shown in Table 3.3, which indicates the size of the anti-incumbent vote at conventions after 1896. There is a clear increase in that vote since 1972 in both parties, but we are left to wonder what the figure for 1968 would have been had Johnson stayed in the race. And there is other, conflicting evidence: Nixon's steamroller over the challenges of Representatives McCloskey and Ashbrook in 1972, Ford's and Carter's overcoming Reagan's and Kennedy's preprimary leads in the polls, and the Republican coronation of 1984.

Perhaps a comment by E. E. Schattschneider in 1942 can give us a framework for understanding recent trends in the Presidential impact on conventions: "The future of American politics is likely to be determined very largely by a triangular tug of war among the

TABLE 3.3. Percentage of votes cast against incumbent Presidents, national conventions, 1900–1984

Year	Incumbent	Democratic	Republican
1900	McKinley	—	0.0
1904	T. Roosevelt	—	0.0
1912	Taft	—	48.4
1916	Wilson	—[a]	—
1924	Coolidge	—	4.0
1932	Hoover	—	2.4
1936	F. D. Roosevelt	—[a]	—
1940	F. D. Roosevelt	14.0	—
1944	F. D. Roosevelt	7.7	—
1948	Truman	25.0	—
1956	Eisenhower	—	0.0
1964	L. B. Johnson	—[a]	—
1972	Nixon	—	0.1
1976	Ford	—	47.5
1980	Carter	36.3	—
1984	Reagan	—	0.1

[a]Nominated by acclamation.

principal forms of political organization in the United States: (1) the presidential parties, (2) the local party bosses, and (3) the pressure groups."[16] The twentieth century has seen a vast increase in Presidential power and a concomitant decline in the power of local bosses, reversing the situation of the previous century, when those local leaders could, and frequently did, deny the incumbent the nomination. If we expand Schattschneider's usage of "pressure groups" to include the more recent rise of candidate organizations (discussed later in this chapter), constituency factions (see Chapter 5), and ideological groups (see Chapter 6), we can see that they have been rising in power in recent decades. Thus after a period of nearly unchallenged Presidential supremacy in the nominating process, due to the weakness of both local party leaders and pressure groups, we are in an era in which the President is still strong but can be effectively challenged by emergent pressure groups.

Indeed, in the first half of the twentieth century the local leaders were sometimes a great asset to an incumbent, as Taft and Truman could testify. With their decline, and with the devolution of power in the party, the President loses some of his special advantages. Sears may see the proliferation of primaries as hurting under-financed challengers, but they hold a sword of Damocles over Presidents as well. It was, after all, the New Hampshire primary that did in Truman in 1952 and Johnson in 1968, and more primary defeats would have destroyed Ford and Carter later.

Since Johnson did not fight for renomination at the 1968 convention, it is unclear whether the trend toward effective challenges to Presidents began in 1968 or in 1976. It is also unclear who, if anyone, is hurt more by the new rules, the ins or the outs. But it seems clear that the present situation of the incumbent can be explained to a great extent by long-term changes in the political equilibrium, which both undercut local leaders and augment the influence of other, newer power centers.

Primaries and the Nomination

If governors, party organization elites, and incumbents have less sway over conventions than they used to, one of the most important loci of power in recent times has been the delegate primary. Table 1.1 shows how primaries have proliferated in recent years, but their role in the process needs further examination in order to determine whether it is all it is said to be. The role of primaries in the Presidential nominating process has always been controversial, from the days when the *New York Times* called the primary "a nursery of obscurities and waggeries" to when Harry Truman called them "eyewash" and Adlai Stevenson said of the process, "All it does is destroy some candidates."[17] A leading authority on primaries, James Davis, counts no fewer than twenty aspirants whose chances for the nomination were destroyed by poor primary showings from 1912 to 1964 and concludes that relying on primaries alone will not get a candidate nominated.[18]

Have primaries become more important as the key to the nomination? One way to answer this is to see whether nominees received a disproportionate number of votes at the convention from

TABLE 3.4. Mean vote percentage received by nominees at contested single-ballot conventions, primary and nonprimary state delegations, 1912–1984 (numbers in parentheses denote number of states in group)

Year	Democratic			Republican		
	Pri-mary	Others	Differ-ence	Pri-mary	Others	Differ-ence
1912	—	—	—	14.2 (13)	73.4 (35)	−59.2
1948	83.3 (14)	73.9 (34)	+ 9.4	—	—	—
1952	—	—	—	41.5 (14)	49.7 (34)	− 8.2
1956	86.2 (18)	63.2 (30)	+23.1	—	—	—
1960	66.4 (16)	45.5 (34)	+20.9	—	—	—
1964	—	—	—	64.9 (14)	72.0 (36)	− 7.1
1968	46.7 (13)	78.2 (37)	−31.5	66.4 (13)	59.1 (37)	+ 7.3
1972	58.8 (20)	48.1 (30)	+10.7	—	—	—
1976	75.7 (26)	76.2 (24)	− 0.5	57.3 (26)	43.9 (24)	+13.4
1980	63.8 (32)	70.1 (18)	− 6.3	—	—	—
1984	53.2 (27)	54.2 (23)	− 1.0	—	—	—

primary states. Here it will be appropriate to analyze contested conventions whose nominations were decided on the first ballot, since a nominee chosen on a later ballot might have received many votes from primary states without having run in them. This gives us the conventions listed in Table 3.4, and the reader should pay particular attention to the third column under each party ("Difference"). If this number has a positive sign, the nominee did better in the primary states; a negative number indicates that the better showing was in the nonprimary states. Before 1968, Democratic nominees tended to do better in primary states, Republican nominees in other states. Starting in 1968 the situation has been reversed in both parties. Why Democratic nominees are increasingly likely to run better in *non*primary states is something that the members of the 1972 school should ponder.

Perhaps the real significance of Table 3.4 is that the absolute value of the figures in the "Difference" columns has shrunk in the Democratic party. In other words, Democratic nominees have been doing about equally well in primary and nonprimary states in recent years. This suggests that a strategy of working only in the primaries has not been the road to victory. However, there is another explanation, related to the proliferation of primaries since 1968. In earlier years, with few primaries, the primary states were often an unrepresentative group. Ten of the thirteen primary states in 1968, for example, were in the Northeast or the Midwest. By 1980, primary states were fairly evenly distributed around the nation. This means that a candidate with a regional appeal—and most nominees in contested races run stronger in some parts of the nation than others—is likely to have done particularly well in one kind of state before 1972 but about equally well in both since then. And this is clearly the case, at least on the Democratic side.

Of course, these data are misleading in a couple of ways. A great deal of anecdotal information tells us that primaries *were* often important, and sometimes rather unimportant, despite the figures in Table 3.4. Barry Goldwater did not run well in the primaries, but the California primary knocked his main opponent, Nelson Rockefeller, out of the race. Richard Nixon ran well in the 1968 primaries, but he had no opposition to speak of in any of them. Jimmy Carter did equally well in both types of states in 1976, but who can deny the importance of the primaries for his victory that year?

The second problem with the data is reflected in the figures in parentheses in Table 3.4. The simple fact is that three-quarters of the delegates in 1980 were selected in states with primaries, and it is almost mathematically impossible to win a nomination today without a string of primary victories. This is especially so in the Democratic party, with its requirements for proportional representation. Moreover, a candidate is unlikely to keep filling the campaign coffers without evidence that there is hope for the candidacy, and the primaries provide a salient means of proving this.

My conclusion, therefore, is that while there is nothing to require a victorious candidate to have run especially well in the primary states, the sheer proliferation of primaries makes this strategy more important today than ever before.

Candidate Organizations

Primaries are the chief vehicle today for sending delegates to the convention, but what happens in the convention hall is another matter. In Chapter 6 we will look at the kind of person who is nominated, but here it is pertinent to discuss the power structure at the convention. One of the most frequent observations about recent conventions is that the power centers are no longer state delegations, where delegates listened to their leaders' instructions about how to vote, but rather the candidates' organizations, which transmit orders to friendly delegates around the auditorium. This is the entity, we are told, that has filled the vacuum left by the decline of party leaders. Moreover, it is suggested that this trend was the result of any or all of the following rules: proportional representation (Mikulski) rules that required delegates to opt for their favorite candidates early; the proliferation of primaries, which accomplished the same thing; changes in rules governing caucuses and conventions, to make them more like candidate-oriented primaries; rules ensuring that delegates would be chosen because of their candidate preference; allowing candidates to veto people who wanted to be their delegates, and other rules governing slate-making; abolition of the unit rule, which encouraged the proliferation of candidate efforts everywhere; and FECA provisions, which may have encouraged more candidacies.[19] Everett Ladd cites Richard Nixon's now-notorious Committee to Re-Elect the President as "the prototypical contemporary electoral organization: it was formed to serve the interests of one man; it placed these above the party's; and its substantial resources enabled it to disregard the party in contesting for the presidency."[20]

This is something that cannot be measured easily with quantitative methods, but such descriptions of recent campaigns did not begin with the 1972 campaign. Indeed, the observations of scholars and journalists indicate that the trend was a long time brewing. Perhaps the earliest harbinger was the campaign for Wendell Willkie in 1940. Donald Bruce Johnson describes the original leaders of the campaign—a young attorney, a journalist, a banker, an industrialist, and a Republican activist—and adds:

Working with these men was a large group of professional public relations experts who made the first great, though uncoordinated, effort by this segment of the population to engineer mass consensus behind a presidential nominee. These men, whose contemporaries and successors today have become essential fixtures in any well-developed political campaign, were as enthusiastic about supporting an articulate businessman for the nomination as were any of the financial leaders of Wall Street. . . .

From its inception the Willkie preconvention movement was spearheaded by two groups which ordinarily played neither an active nor an open role in presidential primary campaigns: the Willkie-for-President Clubs, organized by Oren Root among non-party amateurs who displayed more enthusiasm than local party organizations generated in support of either political party in 1940, and the businessmen, financiers, and publishers, led by the mass distributors of the Willkie saga, *Fortune* and the *Saturday Evening Post.*[21]

Twelve years later, the Eisenhower campaign was another amateurish, candidate-oriented movement to propel a man of ambiguous partisanship into the Republican nomination. While the campaign was led by its share of professionals, David Broder comments:

His election depended only to a minimal degree on the support of Republican party workers; Eisenhower himself felt much closer to the "Citizens for Eisenhower," the independent-minded volunteers who joined in helping nominate and elect him. . . .

His supporters won Texas—which proved to be the key to the nomination—by flooding the precinct caucuses, the county conventions, and finally the state convention with hordes of newly-enlisted amateurs, whose Republican credentials the Taft regulars protested in vain were nonexistent.[22]

Like Willkie, Eisenhower chose as his running-mate a party regular to offset his own image with Republicans, and like Willkie too his campaign was heavily oriented toward the mass media. It was Eisenhower who ran the first televised advertising campaign with the help of a major advertising firm, Batten, Barton, Durstine and Osborn.

John Kennedy was another nominee who ran a highly personalized campaign, led by "those who had survived a decade of Kennedy selection."[23] Broder describes the prototypical Kennedy campaign, his first for public office:

Kennedy won the nomination easily in a ten-man field, exploiting the double tactics so typical of his ambivalent relationship with the party: his father used his funds and his contacts to line up as many of the organization politicians as he could reach; Kennedy and his contemporaries enlisted the amateurs and carried the campaign to voters beyond the grasp of the organization. Six years later, by the time he was ready to reach for the Senate, the "Kennedy organization" in Massachusetts, in which the professional politicians were a distinct minority to the amateurs, was so far superior to anything the faction-ridden state Democratic party could muster that every other office seeker in the state was frantically grabbing for Kennedy's help and coattails. . . .

The point is that, despite his Democratic heritage, despite his personal and family links to some of the established powers in the party, Kennedy won the [presidential] nomination essentially by going outside the organization, using "political amateurs," to round up votes in the primaries and thus forcing the professionals in the "cadre party" to accept him as the nominee.[24]

My final example is again a Republican one, the movement that nominated Barry Goldwater. Robert Novak concluded:

The new Goldwater-style of preconvention politics did not waste time on winning over county and state organizations, but concentrated on actually taking over the county and state organizations by an inundation of the Goldwater volunteers. It was indeed a revolutionary doctrine. It meant that the Goldwater delegates sent to San Francisco would be not merely the run-of-the-mill party workers under the command and bidding of regular party leaders. Here was a new breed of delegate, most of whom had never been to a national convention before. They were going not as a reward for faithful service, not to see the sights of San Francisco, and certainly not to ride the bandwagon of a winner. They were going there for one purpose: to vote for Barry Goldwater.[25]

In a scholarly vein, Aaron Wildavsky presents a similar portrait of the Goldwater delegates.[26]

I have been quoting various authors at length to show that the candidate-centered campaign did not begin in 1972. I have chosen only the most obvious examples, and I have omitted equally candidate-oriented losing nominating campaigns, such as those for Harold Stassen, Estes Kefauver, and Eugene McCarthy. Let me repeat that this is impressionistic evidence, and I know of no way to measure whether campaigns emphasizing the candidate are more prevalent or more likely to win today than they were in 1940, 1952, 1960, or 1964. I believe, however, that I have established that the McGovern-Fraser or Mikulski rules were not required to produce this development.

If the rules did not lead to the advent of the candidate-centered campaign, then what did? It seems reasonable to draw inferences from the most salient features of such campaigns: nonpartisan campaign workers, and campaign staffers whose emphasis was on public relations and mass media. The first characteristic reflects the growing independence of the electorate, the second the rise of a new campaign technology based on the rise of market research, public opinion surveys, and the electronic media.[27] Both in turn are intertwined with the decline of traditional party organizations, whose atrophy freed voters from dependence on party machinery and forced candidates to establish their own campaign networks. As candidates did so, they came to rely even less on the party organization, and a spiraling vicious circle of weak parties and free-wheeling candidates was the result. This seems the most plausible account of the rise of candidate-oriented campaign organizations, consistent with the timing of that development.

Conclusions

After the findings of Chapter 2, it is not surprising to see in this chapter that the power bases within the parties have indeed shifted, from older organizational elites to delegates chosen in primaries and marshaled by candidate-centered organizations. Governors have become less effective at securing delegations committed to the gubernatorial choice among Presidential candidates; incumbent Presidents have been finding it more difficult to secure the nomination easily; primaries have proliferated to the point where they have become a necessity in winning nominations; and candidate-oriented organizations have become the norm, with candidates no longer able to rely on the party machinery in their locality as their organizational base. The only generalization we have been unable to confirm is that national party elites have become less effective at working their will on the convention. This seems true for the Democrats but not for the Republicans, and in either case it might involve a situation like that of the fabled French revolutionary leader who said, "Excuse me, I just saw my people going by, and I must go out and lead them."

Just when did these changes occur? Two of these changes, the weakening of the incumbency advantage and the rise of candidate organizations, seem clearly to have preceded the McGovern-Fraser reforms. One, the rise of primaries, was indisputably caused by those same reforms, however unintentionally. The sapping of gubernatorial strength is less easily categorized and may be the result not of the rules but of the rise in the success rate of insurgent candidacies, which seem correlated with gubernatorial weakness. However, this may only be begging the question, because we should ask why insurgencies have been more successful, and this brings us right back to the heart of the issue addressed in this book—how responsible were the reforms for the new process? If they were responsible, then gubernatorial weakness is an indirect effect of the reforms; if not, then gubernatorial decline is yet another by-product of the secular changes behind the decline of the American political party. It is a matter that will have to await the rest of the analysis of this book.

FOUR

Who Are the Delegates?

I f the basis on which delegates are chosen and led has changed, then we should expect that the delegates themselves will be different from what they were. If so, then it should not be surprising that these changes would be among the most controversial of all. Being a delegate to a national nominating convention entitles one to both status and a modicum of power, and as one type of citizen replaces another as delegate, tempers are bound to flare up. Nor is this only a matter of whose ox is gored, for more disinterested analysts may applaud or lament the effect of this transition on the parties or on the political process. My task here is a bit narrower: to ascertain whether delegates are indeed different from delegates of the past and, if so, when these differences first arose. In particular, I shall examine whether they are demographically different, whether they have less convention experience, whether high public officials are less likely to be delegates, and whether delegates are less likely to vote as a bloc than they used to be.

Demography of the Delegates

Among the most controversial of the reforms were those involving affirmative action, aimed at increasing the proportions of young, black, and female delegates. Indeed, the whole modern reform cycle began with concern in the Democratic party in the 1960s over the exclusion of blacks from many Southern delegations. Despite Republican attacks against the resulting Democratic

59

"quotas," the Republican party also made efforts to increase the representation of such groups at their convention in 1972. It will not be difficult to demonstrate that in 1972 the representation of those groups, as compared with their presence in the party at large, indeed increased.

The phrase "as compared with their presence in the party at large" is crucial. We might find, for example, that blacks are increasingly represented among Democratic convention delegates, but that may be because blacks *in general* have become more Democratic since the early 1960s. Therefore I shall continually compare a group's share of the delegates with its share of the party masses, as measured by self-identified party members in national surveys. In doing so, I shall utilize a measure of over- or underrepresentation, by dividing the pertinent group's share of delegates by its share of the party masses. If the resulting number is exactly 1, then the group is represented at the convention in exactly the ratio that it is part of the party's mass base. If the number is less than 1, the group is underrepresented at the convention, and if it is greater than 1, the group is overrepresented in the sense that its share of the delegates is greater than its proportion of the masses. Note that "overrepresented" and "underrepresented" are intended here as objective terms and carry no pejorative connotation.

Women

Ever since the turn of the twentieth century, women have been present but grossly underrepresented at both parties' national conventions.[1] While women have long comprised a majority of both parties' mass bases, women being more likely than men to identify with a party, not until 1972 were they more than one-quarter of the delegates at either party's convention.[2] Table 4.1 shows clearly that feminine representation at Democratic conventions took a quantum leap in 1972 and that the party's plan to give women equal representation in 1980 and 1984 was successful. However, the mass data of the table also show that the party has a long way to go before women are represented *proportionally* among the delegates. Table 4.1 also shows that although there was a gradual increase in women's representation at Republican conventions, 1972 was the turning point. In 1984, concern over the "gender gap" and the absence of any intraparty battles helped produce an unprecedented level of women's participation.

TABLE 4.1. **Women as percentage of national convention delegates and of party masses, both major parties, 1952–1984**

	Democratic			Republican		
Year	Delegates	Masses	Del. / Mass[a]	Delegates	Masses	Del. / Mass[a]
1952	13	54	.24	11	57	.19
1956	12	54	.22	16	61	.26
1960	9	56	.16	15	57	.26
1964	13	57	.23	18	58	.31
1968	13	59	.22	16	54	.30
1972	40	61	.66	29	59	.49
1976	33	63	.52	31	62	.50
1980	49	61	.80	29	58	.50
1984	50	58	.86	44	52	.85

SOURCES: See note 2 for this chapter.
[a] Percentage of delegates divided by percentage of masses.

Blacks

Blacks too were grossly underrepresented at conventions of the main party of their choice, the Democrats, until 1972. Table 4.2 shows that even since 1972 they have been underrepresented.[3] So few blacks have been Republicans in recent years that it is easy for the Republican party to represent its few nonwhites proportionally. For the Democrats, the increase in black delegates had begun in 1968, undoubtedly as a result of earlier civil rights rules, but the effects of the McGovern-Fraser rules are clear.

Young People

Unlike race and sex, age is a quantitative variable that can be measured in various ways—mean, median, intervals, and so forth. The most complete data sets for recent years analyze the percentages of delegates age thirty and under, or twenty-nine and under, and that is how I shall analyze age.[4] For the Democrats, the results in Table 4.3 are similar to those in Tables 4.1 and 4.2: gross underrepresentation of young people before 1972, a mammoth change

TABLE 4.2. Blacks as percentage of national convention delegates and of party masses, both major parties, 1952–1984

Year	Democratic			Republican		
	Delegates	Masses	Del. / Mass[a]	Delegates	Masses	Del. / Mass[a]
1952	2	11	.18	3	5	0.60
1964	2	14	.14	1	3	0.33
1968	5	18	.28	2	1	2.00
1972	15	17	.88	4	3	1.33
1976	11	17	.65	3	1	3.00
1980	15	21	.71	3	2	1.50
1984	18	24	.75	4	2	2.00

SOURCES: See note 3 for this chapter.
[a]Percentage of delegates divided by percentage of masses.

that year, and a subsequent drop-off, but not to the pre-1972 levels. The Republican trend is a bit less clear. Part A (age thirty and under) of Table 4.3 is similar to the Democratic trend, but Part B (age twenty-nine and under) shows a jump occurring in 1968. Here I should note that the CBS News data of the table are contradicted by the findings of other scholars, which show the 1968 delegate proportion in Part B as much lower. Indeed, they are contradicted by CBS News' own data in Part A.[5] Whenever the increase began, as with the Democrats it has dropped off since 1972. It may be worth adding at this point that, as with women, in recent years the Democrats have provided young people with more representation than the Republicans have.

My conclusion, which will be one of the less surprising in this book, is that the McGovern-Fraser reforms and their aftermath in both parties indeed changed the demography of both parties' national conventions. This is an area in which only modest change had preceded the 1972 conventions, and one which is clearly affected by changes in formal rules. On another level, however, we can question the *political* significance of these changes, and I shall do so at the end of this chapter.

TABLE 4.3. Young people as percentage of national convention delegates and of party masses, both major parties, 1948–1984

Year	Democratic			Republican		
	Delegates	Masses	Del. / Mass[a]	Delegates	Masses	Del. / Mass[a]
A. Ages 18–30						
1968	3	15	0.20	1	14	0.07
1972	24	24	1.00	8	19	0.42
1976	19	26	0.73	7	21	0.33
1980	13	23	0.57	5	25	0.20
B. Ages 18–29						
1948	1	20	0.05	1	13	0.08
1968	3	13	0.23	4	13	0.31
1972	22	23	0.96	8	18	0.44
1976	15	24	0.63	7	20	0.35
1980	11	20	0.52	5	23	0.22
1984	8	23	0.35	4	34	0.12

SOURCES: See note 4 for this chapter.
[a] Percentage of delegates divided by percentage of masses.

Experience of the Delegates

Have the new rules, especially those that restrict the ability of party leaders to select delegates, produced an increase in the proportion of delegates who are attending their first convention? A number of scholars and journalists have gathered the data necessary to answer this question, and their findings appear in Table 4.4.[6] The Democratic data clearly indicate the effects of the rules in producing a bumper crop of neophyte delegates after 1968. The drop in newcomers in 1984 might similarly be attributed to the effects of the Hunt Commission's provisions for party and elected officials, although I have no data on whether such delegates were especially likely to have attended prior conventions.

TABLE 4.4. Percentage of delegates attending their first convention, 1952–1984

Year	Democratic	Republican
1952	67	64
1956	67	65
1960	58	61
1964	54	66
1968	67	66
1972	83	78
1976	80	78
1980	87	84
1984	74	69

SOURCES: See note 6 for this chapter.

The Republican data in Table 4.4 parallel the Democratic trends and raise some questions. We might attribute the rise in Republican neophytes in 1972 to the party's attempt to bring to the convention more women, blacks, and young people, as shown in Tables 4.1, 4.2, and 4.3, but why did a similar drive that dramatically increased the proportion of women delegates in 1984 not produce a similar increase? Indeed, 1984 marked the lowest Republican figure in Table 4.4 since 1968. And why were the Republican figures for 1976 and 1980 so high? The answer might have to do with the fact that the 1976 and 1980 Republican conventions followed hotly contested nominating races. Nominating contests seem to produce high delegate turnover, presumably because a candidate's supporters are eager to exclude convention veterans who do not support the candidate in question. The lowest Democratic figure in Table 4.4 is for the only uncontested convention in the period, and the lowest Republican figure was also for an uncontested convention. While the Republican races in 1976 and 1980 might explain the high figures in the table, it should be stressed that they are considerably higher than the figures for the contested years of 1952 and 1964. Is this evidence of the effects of the decline of party? If so, then why is the last figure in the sequence so low?

For a couple of reasons, then, the figure for 1984 is anomalous. Without it we might conclude that the proliferation of primaries had a major impact on Republican delegate turnover and leave it at that. With it the table has one striking bit of inexplicable data.

Officeholders as Delegates

In Chapter 3 I discussed the decline in the power of party leaders at national conventions. One tangible piece of evidence of that decline is the decreasing proportion of such leaders who attend national conventions. There was no better symbol of this change than the exclusion of Chicago's Mayor Richard Daley from the 1972 Democratic convention. The McGovern-Fraser rules explicitly outlawed provisions for ex-officio delegates chosen solely by virtue of other offices held; they also limited the number of delegates to be chosen by party committee to 10 percent of the delegation.[7] Moreover, there have been longer-term trends consistent with the argument of the party-decline school. If candidate-oriented factions have replaced party leaders as the controlling force at conventions, as discussed in Chapter 3, then backers of the winning candidate in a state can deprive party leaders of seats on the delegation if they do not support that candidate. Furthermore, there may be a circular process whereby, as leaders lose power, they find attendance at conventions less attractive because voting for a certain candidate may alienate others in the party and thus endanger their own position; they therefore cease trying to become delegates, and consequently abdicate power still further.

Who are the highest officeholders? For the sake of convenience, I shall define them as governors and members of Congress. It is obvious that other officials—state party chairpersons, mayors, state legislators, and others—have also been important party leaders. But limitations of time and information are prohibitive, and governors and members of Congress are surely disproportionately represented in the party leadership and on the whole are more important than other groups of officials.

There are divergent opinions as to what happened to the convention participation of such officials. Jeane Kirkpatrick and Austin Ranney, the latter relying on inaccurate data supplied by the

TABLE 4.5. Percentage of high Democratic officeholders who were delegates to national conventions, 1928–1984

Year	Governors	Senators	Representatives
1928	42.9	52.2	—a
1932	63.0	55.3	—a
1936	60.5	81.2	—a
1940	60.0	60.9	—a
1944	81.8	62.1	—a
1948	62.5	57.8	15.1
1952	82.6	76.0	18.1
1956	70.4	69.4	28.1
1960	85.3	72.3	44.5
1964	79.4	71.6	50.0
1968	91.7	66.7	35.8
1972	66.7	35.2	14.9
1976	44.4	18.0	14.6
1980	74.2	13.8	13.5
1984	82.9	62.2	66.4

SOURCES: See note 12 for this chapter.
aData not compiled.

staff of the Winograd Commission, argue that the rules led to less participation.[8] John Stewart suggests that state parties went beyond the letter of the reforms and that in 1972 only 1.7 percent of the delegates were chosen by party committees.[9] Denis Sullivan and associates charge that the 1972 Democratic delegates were equally as likely as those in 1968 to hold party or public office.[10] Kenneth Bode and Carol Casey acknowledge that participation dropped in 1972, but attribute this to elected officials' desire not to be associated with the McGovern candidacy and to many party leaders' support of Edmund Muskie, who lost.[11]

Table 4.5 presents the rates of convention attendance of Democratic officeholders in recent decades.[12] The rules seem at first glance to be associated with steep declines in the participation rates of all three groups. A second look, however, suggests that the gubernatorial decline is not as clear. Certainly the attendance rate of governors in 1976 was unusually low, the lowest since 1928. However, the rates in 1972, 1980, and 1984 were not especially low: discounting the unusually low rates in 1928 and 1976, the mean rate from 1932 through 1968 was 73.7 percent, and the mean of the 1972, 1980, and 1984 rates was 74.6 percent. For all the hullabaloo about excluding top party officials, the most powerful official of all (see Chapter 3) did not suffer any significant attrition.

Skeptics will no doubt cite the rules for the respectable gubernatorial attendance rates in 1980 and 1984. The Winograd and Hunt commissions expanded each delegation's size to accommodate party and elected officials.[13] But even before these rules were adopted the gubernatorial attendance rate in 1972 was still 66.7 percent, only a slight drop from earlier decades. More striking is the fact that the Winograd rules had no effect at all on the attendance rates of members of Congress, which continued to decline. This suggests that congressional participation was not wholly affected by the formal rules; after all, attendance of House members in 1948 and 1952 was as low as some recent rates (on the other hand, the Hunt rules seem to have had the desired impact). What we may have been seeing in recent years is a manifestation of the celebrated concentration of members of Congress on getting reelected.[14] After all, if officeholders are single-mindedly interested in their own reelection prospects, they may well resist getting involved in a Presidential nominating battle that might antagonize many party stalwarts in their district. As Representative Geraldine Ferraro put it three years before her Vice-Presidential nomination, "The convention is most important but if I have the choice of whether I'm a delegate to the convention or going to lose votes and make my reelection to Congress more difficult three months later, then rest assured that I'm going to look out for my reelection."[15] This may explain why House members' attendance rates began dropping in 1968 and not in 1972. It may also explain why senators running for reelection in 1984 were far less likely than their colleagues to become delegates that year; moreover, none of the five who did so endorsed a Presidential candidate.

Data for the Republicans provide a test of the Democratic trends, for the Republican party did not adopt the McGovern-Fraser reforms or subsequent rules. Table 4.6 shows that the attendance rate of Republican governors declined substantially and almost mono-

TABLE 4.6. Percentage of high Republican officeholders who were delegates to national conventions, 1928–1984

Year	Governors	Senators	Representatives
1928	40.7	42.9	—[a]
1932	47.4	45.8	—[a]
1936	50.0	12.0	—[a]
1940	50.0	26.1	—[a]
1944	53.8	40.5	—[a]
1948	45.8	41.2	5.3
1952	52.0	40.0	7.5
1956	71.4	53.2	11.9
1960	93.8	48.6	18.4
1964	87.5	48.5	23.0
1968	88.5	55.6	31.0
1972	80.0	50.0	27.0
1976	69.2	56.8	37.2
1980	73.7	63.4	39.6
1984	86.7	54.5	43.4

SOURCES: See note 12 for this chapter.
[a] Data not compiled.

tonically from 1960 to 1980, and this is the most impressive evidence for the party-decline thesis presented in that table or in Table 4.5. However, the rate rose substantially in the consensual 1984 convention. There was no significant change in the attendance rate of Republican Senators from 1956 to 1984, and there was a gradual increase in the attendance of House members over at least the past three decades. This calls into question the reelection hypothesis that I used to explain Democratic congressional trends, unless one were to argue either that Democratic members of Congress are more concerned than Republicans with reelection or that Republican Presidential races are less divisive than Democratic contests. Neither argument has much surface plausibility.

Before leaving this topic, it is necessary to consider Bode and Casey's argument that attendance is down because leaders back the wrong candidate. Of course, in previous eras a party leader would be selected as a delegate regardless of whom he or she endorsed, and this change is significant in itself. But do states that support insurgent candidates send fewer high elected officials to the conventions than states that back establishment candidates? As in Chapter 3, I shall designate as insurgents Goldwater in 1964, all of Humphrey's rivals in 1968, McGovern, Wallace, and Chisholm in 1972, Reagan in 1976, Kennedy in 1980, and Hart and Jackson in 1984. (Recall that I do not include Carter in 1976 in this category because by mid-June the party establishment was behind him.)

But looking at the raw data is not enough. Some state parties, such as the Hawaii Republicans and the Wyoming Democrats, always seem to send all their high officials to the conventions, while others, such as Alabama Democrats and North Dakota Republicans, almost never do. So I shall compare what percentage of a state's high officials—governors and members of Congress—were delegates in a given year with the mean percentage for that state for all years from 1964 to 1984. Then we will know whether the attendance rate was unusually high or low.

Table 4.7 provides the data, and for all years except 1984, backers of insurgents sent fewer high officials to the conventions than did supporters of establishment candidates. However, the last column of Table 4.7 shows that when compared with the states' mean attendance rates, it is apparent that only for the Republicans in 1976 and the Democrats in 1984 was the difference between the two groups substantial, and in the latter case the insurgent states had a *higher* than expected attendance by high officials. This suggests that the decline in the attendance of elected officials cannot be explained by recent party insurgencies.

There are several conclusions to draw here, and they do not provide us with a clear-cut picture of what has happened to the attendance rates of high elected officials:

1. Until 1984, Democratic members of Congress, but not governors, sharply reduced their attendance at conventions. The Winograd rules did nothing to reverse this.
2. The three categories of Republican officeholders show three different trends: less gubernatorial attendance until 1984, more House members' attendance, and no change in senatorial attendance.

TABLE 4.7. Mean percentage of a state party's governor and members of Congress who attended national conventions as delegates, by type of candidate supported by the delegation and compared with the state's mean 1964–1984 attendance rate by such officials, for selected conventions (numbers in parentheses denote number of states in category)

	Mean for that convention	1964–1984 Mean	Difference
A. Republicans, 1964			
Insurgents (27)	39	43	− 4
Evenly divided (3)	41	54	−13
Establishment (12)	51	50	+ 1
B. Democrats, 1968			
Insurgents (11)	47	36	+11
Establishment (38)	59	45	+14
C. Democrats, 1972			
Insurgents (37)	26	40	−14
Evenly divided (1)	29	36	− 7
Establishment (10)	47	53	− 6
D. Republicans, 1976			
Insurgents (22)	31	47	−16
Establishment (25)	60	50	+10
E. Democrats, 1980			
Insurgents (10)	18	44	−26
Evenly divided (2)	50	61	−11
Establishment (38)	20	42	−22
F. Democrats, 1984			
Insurgents (20)	77	44	+33
Evenly divided (1)	100	100	0
Establishment (29)	59	40	+19

Note: States without any governor or member of Congress from that party in that year are omitted from that year's calculations.

3. For the most part, the declines in attendance cannot be explained by the fact that party leaders tend to back establishment candidates and sometimes see their state delegations won by insurgents.

This leads me to conclude that these trends are highly office-specific, with different offices displaying different trends within each party. Changes in the rules, as well as longer-term trends, seem to have different impacts on different offices, and it is not difficult to imagine why. Some offices (notably the governorship) are closer to the core of party leadership than others, and some (notably U.S. Representative) seem to have developed their own incentive structures divorced from other political currents. The net effect is that it is all too easy to overgeneralize about these matters, and scholars of the process should tread carefully in this area.

The Unity of Delegations

Once the delegates are selected, is their recent behavior substantially different from how delegates used to behave? An important part of the answer, the persistence of cleavages over time, deserves a chapter in itself, and I shall deal with it in Chapter 5. Here I am concerned with how unified the state delegation is, for a number of recent Democratic rules changes would seem to encourage divisions within delegations. First was the abolition of the unit rule, which had required that the entire delegation vote the way its majority wanted it to. This was abolished at the 1968 convention and then permanently repealed by the McGovern-Fraser Commission. The Mikulski proportional representation rules almost guaranteed that each delegation would be divided in a contested convention. Moreover, affirmative-action rules that provided for black representation in Southern delegations introduced not only racial but also political diversity, as a Charles Evers and a John Stennis are likely to support different candidates. But the party-decline school might also predict such a trend. As long ago as 1960, Paul David and his colleagues argued that the loss of power of statewide party leaders would mean less unified delegations.[16]

There are several ways to measure the unity of delegations, and the study by David and his colleagues provides three, which I have adapted for this study.[17] Two of these measures are quite straight-forward. One is simply the percentage of state delegations that voted unanimously. Of course, this is a rather crude measure, lumping together the most fractionalized delegations with those that divided 99 to 1. The second measure is the "Index of Candidate Agreement," or the percentage of a delegation's vote going to whoever received the most votes from that delegation. A unanimous delegation has an index of 100.0, while one that gave nobody more than five of its thirty votes would get an index of 16.7. For each convention, the mean of all states' Indexes of Candidate Agreement was computed.

The third measure, inspired by the David study but adapted here to a different form, is what I shall call the "Index of Delegation Unity." Assume that, at the convention, Candidate Jones wins with x percent of the vote. We can conceptualize two extreme patterns of relationships among delegations. At one extreme, every delegation is unanimous for Jones *or* one of his or her opponents, and delegations casting x percent of the total vote opt for Jones. Here the battle is *between* delegations. At the other extreme, every delegation casts x percent of its vote for Jones. Here the battle is *within* delegations.

There are two variables here: the unity of each delegation, and its support for the winning candidate. We can measure the unity of each delegation by the percentage of votes going to the candidate whom it favors the most (the aforementioned Index of Candidate Agreement); call this variable m. We can measure the delegation's support for the *winning* candidate by the percentage of its votes that are cast for him or her; call this variable n. Since variable n must be less than or equal to variable m (less than m if Jones is not the delegation's most favored candidate, equal to m if he or she is most favored), we can subtract the mean of n from the mean of m for the numerator of the new index.

If the fight is *between* delegations, every delegation will be unanimous; the mean of m will be 100 percent. In a contested convention, only some delegations will give Jones their votes; the mean of n will approximate x, the percentage of votes Jones receives from the convention at large. (It will only approximate it because delegations are of different sizes, although here we treat them equally.) If the fight is *within* delegations, every delegation will be divided, with Jones receiving x percent from each of them. The mean of m

will equal x, and the mean of n will equal x. In this case, the mean of m minus the mean of n will equal x minus x, or 0.

The denominator of the new index will be 100 minus the mean of n, which equals the mean of m minus the mean of n when the battle is between delegations. Therefore the Index of Delegation Unity, expressed as a percentage, equals

$$100 \times (\text{mean of } m - \text{mean of } n)/(100 - \text{mean of } n).$$

When the battle is entirely between delegations, the index will equal $100 \times (100 - \text{mean of } n)/(100 - \text{mean of } n)$, or 100 percent. When the battle is entirely within delegations, the index equals $100 \times (x - x)/(100 - \text{mean of } n)$, or 0 percent.

In Tables 4.8 and 4.12, then, the Index of Delegation Unity should be interpreted as follows:

1. The higher the index, the more the battle is *between* delegations.
2. The lower the index, the more the battle is *within* delegations.
3. Fifty percent represents the situation wherein the two components are equally mixed.

All these measures are constructed so that the higher the number, the more unified the delegations. Therefore we should expect to see all indexes declining in recent years, and if the 1972 school is correct, the sharpest decline for the Democrats should be in 1968, with the inauguration of affirmative-action requirements and the abolition of the unit rule.

The Democrats

Table 4.8 shows the three indexes for the first ballots of all contested conventions since 1896, and 1968 certainly appears to be a watershed. The first and third indexes plunged to unprecedented depths that year and have not recovered. While the drop in the Index of Candidate Agreement has not been nearly as dramatic—unlike the other indexes it should usually exceed 50—the 1968 index was lower than any previous one except for 1920 and 1952, and subsequent indexes have been lower. But note also that for all three indexes the scores from 1952 to 1960 were also lower than most of the previous ones, indicating a moderate trend before the rules were changed and some evidence for the party-decline thesis.

Which rules change—abolition of the unit rule, proportional representation, or forced racial integration—was most important

TABLE 4.8. Indexes of delegation cohesion, first ballot of contested
Democratic conventions, 1896–1984

Year	Percent of delegations voting unanimously	Index of candidate agreement	Index of delegation unity
1896	60.0	85.6	81.4
1904	80.0	90.7	77.0
1912	72.9	90.6	81.9
1920	45.8	75.3	64.3
1924	77.1	92.7	86.6
1932	85.4	95.7	84.4
1948	83.3	97.8	90.6
1952	50.0	78.8	71.1
1956	54.2	90.1	64.9
1960	58.0	86.0	70.4
1968	6.0	78.9	29.9
1972	14.0	68.7	34.2
1976	12.0	78.6	10.8
1980	4.0	69.5	10.0
1984	2.0	59.4	12.2

in effecting this dramatic development? Tables 4.9, 4.10, and 4.11 compare the means of these indexes for the five contested conventions from 1968 to 1984 with the means of the indexes for the three previous contested conventions, from 1952 to 1960. I might have used the 1948 convention, but Table 4.8 shows that its delegations were unusually cohesive. The 1952–1960 era was rather stable in terms of delegation unity.

The reader should also note that I have dropped the Index of Delegation Unity, which strictly speaking is a measure of the conflict pattern in the convention as a whole. Therefore it would be misleading to apply it to subgroups of states, and consequently for such subgroups we will be observing only the percentage of unanimous delegations and, more useful, the Index of Candidate Agreement.

Table 4.9 singles out the states that had the unit rule in 1956, the midpoint of the earlier period under investigation, and winner-

TABLE 4.9. Changes in indexes of delegation cohesion, contested Democratic conventions, 1952–1984, by rules changes

	Unit rule (N = 12)	Winner-take-all selection procedures (N = 5)	Both (N = 2)	Neither (N = 29)
A. Percentage of delegations voting unanimously				
1952–1960	88.9	80.0	100.0	32.2
1968–1984	5.0	16.0	10.0	4.8
Change	−83.9	−64.0	− 90.0	−27.4
B. Index of Candidate Agreement				
1952–1960	93.9	91.6	100.0	79.4
1968–1984	72.9	74.8	63.7	69.4
Change	−21.0	−16.8	− 36.3	−10.0

TABLE 4.10. Changes in indexes of delegation cohesion, contested Democratic conventions, 1952–1984, by region within selected rules categories

	Unit rule		Neither	
	Non-South (N = 8)	South (N = 4)	Non-South (N = 25)	South (N = 4)
A. Percentage of delegations voting unanimously				
1952–1960	83.3	100.0	33.3	25.0
1968–1984	5.0	5.0	4.0	10.0
Change	−78.3	− 95.0	−29.3	−15.0
B. Index of Candidate Agreement				
1952–1960	90.9	100.0	78.9	83.1
1968–1984	72.2	74.1	68.2	76.4
Change	−18.7	− 25.9	−10.7	− 6.7

TABLE 4.11. Changes in indexes of delegation cohesion, contested Democratic conventions, 1952–1984, by political culture for non-Southern states without unit rule or winner-take-all selection procedures in 1956

	Individualistic (N = 12)	Moralistic (N = 11)
A. Percentage of delegations voting unanimously		
1952–1960	36.1	33.3
1968–1984	5.0	3.6
Change	−31.1	−29.7
B. Index of Candidate Agreement		
1952–1960	82.6	77.6
1968–1984	71.4	65.6
Change	−11.2	−12.0

take-all delegate selection procedures that year as well.[18] The first point to be stressed is that cohesion declined *regardless* of the category we are examining. Both parts of the table show that the states with *both* features in 1956 experienced the greatest drop in delegation unity thereafter, and those with *neither* feature experienced the smallest drop. Moreover, both parts of the table show that states with the unit rule had a greater drop than winner-take-all states, although on the more sensitive Index of Candidate Agreement the difference is slight.

The third explanation was the racial integration of Southern delegations, so I hypothesize that, controlling for the other rules changes just cited, Southern delegations underwent a greater drop in unity than non-Southern delegations did. (I am defining the South here as the eleven former Confederate states.) Since I have just established that the winner-take-all and unit rule changes were important, any analysis of regional variations must control for those other variables. Unfortunately, when this is done some of the resulting categories include too few states to make a regional comparison meaningful. But I am able to compare Southern and non-Southern states in the "unit rule" and "neither" categories in Table

4.10. The drop in Southern cohesion was greater than that in non-Southern cohesion only among the unit-rule states, which means that racial integration was not a major cause of the decline in unity for at least four of the Southern states.

If David and his colleagues were correct and the decline in the power of state party leaders was a contributing factor to the trend I am discussing, we should expect to see more of a decline in delegation unity among "machine" states than others. Here it is useful to divide the non-Southern states into "machine" states and others, and one useful typology is Daniel Elazar's. Elazar's "individualistic" political culture is based on a politics of material incentives closely resembling machine politics, while his "moralistic" culture is based on issues and ideologies and suggestive of antimachine reform politics; a third culture defined by Elazar is the "traditionalistic," based on deference and located primarily in the South.[19] In order to control for changes already discussed and still have decent numbers of states in both categories, I shall look only at the non-Southern "neither" category (i.e., neither the unit rule nor winner-take-all selection procedures in 1956). Table 4.11 indicates that there was little difference between individualistic and moralistic states in the degree to which their cohesion declined, and on the Index of Candidate Agreement the small difference was in the opposite of the expected direction. The party-decline thesis apparently does not help us understand this development.

Finally, I performed a multiple regression analysis using the change in the mean of the Index of Candidate Agreement from the 1952–1960 period to the 1968–1984 era as the dependent variable. The independent variables, all dummy variables, were the 1956 unit rule, 1956 winner-take-all procedures, individualistic culture, and Southern location. The result was that, controlling for the other variables, the unit rule was by far the most highly correlated with the drop in cohesion, which is consistent with my other findings. I conclude that the drop in the unity of delegations at Democratic conventions was an across-the-board phenomenon but that changes in the rules, notably the abolition of the unit rule beginning in 1968, contributed disproportionately to that effect.

The Republicans

Table 4.12 replicates Table 4.8 for the Republicans, and it is clear that the post-1960 decline in the indexes for the Democrats

TABLE 4.12. Indexes of delegation cohesion, first ballot of contested
Republican conventions, 1912–1976

Year	Percent of delegations voting unanimously	Index of candidate agreement	Index of delegation unity
1912	39.6	88.0	71.9
1916	29.2	64.4	47.2
1920	35.4	78.7	65.3
1940	35.4	68.3	51.3
1948	25.0	71.1	51.5
1952	20.8	79.8	61.7
1964	44.0	87.5	58.2
1968	34.0	82.2	54.4
1976	26.0	80.5	60.4

did not appear in the Republican party. In fact, some of the highest indexes of all occurred during the three most recent contested conventions, especially for the Index of Candidate Agreement.

To some extent, this finding only reconfirms the argument of the 1972 school that rules changes were responsible for the decline in Democratic delegation cohesion, because the Republicans did not adopt most of these changes. The Republican party had no unit rule to abolish, has not required proportional representation, and has made no major affirmative-action effort regarding race. On the other hand, in some states proportional representation was written into state law and affected both parties, so the stable or increased Republican delegation cohesion is somewhat anomalous.

One likely explanation for this paradox will require getting ahead of the story. In Chapter 5, I shall demonstrate that the main ideological rift within the Republican party has assumed a highly regional form, with the Northeast on the left end of the party and the Southeast and continental Far West at the right pole. This suggests that the party has seen a phalanx of united liberal states against a line of equally unified conservative states. This in turn suggests that ideology may have replaced machine rule as a unifying force within Republican delegations. Therefore the trend toward delegation disunity apparent among the Democrats may have been offset in the case of the Republicans by the force of ideology.

If this is so, we might expect that the greatest increase in cohesion would have occurred among the most ideological states. Of course, in the current period the most ideological states are the most cohesive, since my measure of ideology (to be developed in Chapter 5) is based on the mean vote percentage that a delegation gave to the liberal or the conservative side. The more cohesive a delegation was, and if that cohesion was consistently for one ideological position, the more ideological I consider it. But here I am considering only the *change* in the indexes of cohesion over time. Table 4.13 uses as a measure of ideology the mean percentage of votes the state gave to the conservative side of key votes from 1964 through 1976. Here I have aggregated the 1940, 1948, and 1952 conventions and compared the mean with that of the 1964, 1968, and 1976 contests. While some of the categories are quite small, the three groups that saw the greatest rise in both indexes of dele-

TABLE 4.13. Changes in indexes of delegation cohesion at contested Republican conventions, 1940–1976, by 1964–1976 ideological score (the higher the ideological score, the more conservative the state; numbers in the last two columns represent the change in the index from the 1940–1952 mean to the 1964–1976 mean)

Ideological score	Number of states	Percentage of delegations voting unanimously	Index of candidate agreement
90–100	13	+28.2	+14.9
80–89.9	11	+15.1	+20.0
70–79.9	3	−11.1	+ 8.6
60–69.9	4	+ 8.3	+ 6.9
50–59.9	5	0.0	+ 2.4
40–49.9	2	0.0	+ 3.9
30–39.9	0	—	—
20–29.9	4	−33.4	+ 2.2
10–19.9	4	−16.6	− 4.7
0–9.9	2	+33.3	+17.9

TABLE 4.14. Changes in indexes of delegation cohesion at contested
Republican conventions, 1940–1976, by ideology as measured by
1964–1976 ideological score (numbers in the last two columns
represent the change in the index from the 1940–1952 mean to the
1964–1976 mean)

Ideological score	Number of states	Percentage of delegations voting unanimously	Index of candidate agreement
0–9.9, 90–100 (most ideological)	15	+28.9	+15.7
10–19.9, 80–89.9	15	+ 6.7	+13.4
20–79.9 (least ideological)	18	− 7.4	+ 3.3

gation cohesion were at the most conservative or most liberal end
of the spectrum. Other categories saw little increase, or even a decline, in the indexes.

Readers who are troubled by the small numbers of states in the
categories of Table 4.13 will prefer Table 4.14, which collapses the
categories of Table 4.13 in such a way that states are grouped by
how ideologically consistent they are; here I am ignoring whether
they are liberal or conservative. For example, the "most ideological" category of Table 4.13 combines the very liberal (0 to 9.9) and
very conservative (90 to 100) groupings of Table 4.13; the "least
ideological" category combines those relatively middle-of-the-road
states with scores between 20 and 80. I have chosen those cutoff
points to ensure roughly equal numbers of states in each new category. Clearly, the more ideological a state was, the more likely it
was to experience an increase in cohesion.

I conclude that the Republicans, without most of the rules
changes adopted by the Democrats, experienced no significant
drop in delegation cohesion. Moreover, any decline that might
have occurred was probably arrested by the strikingly regional
nature of Republican party factionalism, which tends to unify
states against others in other regions.

Implications

Conflict apparently takes a radically different form within each major party. At the typical Democratic convention, each state is to some extent a battleground for conflicting forces, somewhat of a microcosm of the nation, and most delegations go to the convention substantially divided. At the typical Republican convention, states tend to be far more unified, and the battle is to a much greater extent a contest of regions. In Chapter 5, there are maps of each party's cleavage structure (Figures 5.1 and 5.2), and the reader will see that the Democratic liberal states are geographically dispersed, with nine in the Northeast, eight in the Midwest, and eleven in the Far West. In the Republican party, however, the liberal states are clustered, with eleven out of twenty-one in the Northeast and six others in the Midwest. That the Republican party is more regionally divided than the Democratic party can be shown with standardized ideological scores to be used in Chapter 5. The Southeast is the most conservative region in both parties and will not be considered here. Elsewhere, the mean Northeastern, Midwestern, and Far Western states have Democratic conservative scores of $-.59$, $-.16$ and $-.45$ respectively; in the Republican party, those mean scores are -1.13, $-.10$ and $+.47$ respectively. While I would not argue that region is a *cause* of Republican factionalism, because the issues have not been explicitly regional, region is a strong *correlate* of that party's division—so strong that it is more logical for that party to have unified state delegations than for the Democrats to do so.

One tactical consequence of this difference is that Democratic candidates should be tempted to run campaigns in every state, even those relatively unfriendly, in order to pick up delegates. After all, even a defeat at a state primary, caucus, or convention will produce a few delegates from a divided delegation. In 1972, for example, George McGovern won votes from all but three states, and Jimmy Carter won votes from every delegation in 1976 and 1980. Edward Kennedy's forces even contested the Georgia primary in 1980.[20] There are, however, two constraints on such activity. One is money; candidates with scarce resources are unlikely to want to spend a lot to go into a state where the payoff is likely to be only a couple of delegates. Another is the fear of being regarded as a loser after entering a few contests and emerging with only a handful of delegates. This could be devastating to one's image in the media and one's ability to raise more funds.

On the Republican side, candidates with clear factional identities should be tempted, in Barry Goldwater's words, to go hunting where the ducks are. This means a Sunbelt strategy for conservatives and a Frostbelt emphasis for liberals. In the Northeast and Midwest in 1976, Gerald Ford won 75 percent of the primaries and carried 79 percent of the delegates; Ronald Reagan meanwhile won 70 percent of the primaries and 72 percent of the delegates from the Southeast and Far West. The only states where Reagan lost primaries in 1980 were in the Northeast and Midwest. Of course, a candidate must campaign outside his or her citadel in order to amass enough votes to win the nomination and to show that he or she has a truly national appeal. To write off any part of the nation, as Goldwater demonstrated, is to create a self-fulfilling prophecy that one has limited appeal. Moreover, it deprives the voters in that region of a real choice in the nominating battle.

Conclusions

In this discussion of delegates, I have demonstrated that changes in the rules affected Democratic delegates in three important ways —they are more young, black, and female than they used to be, they have less experience at prior conventions, and they are less likely to vote as teams with the rest of their delegations. As for governors and members of Congress, the former still attend Democratic conventions at about the same rate as they used to, while until 1984 the latter were staying home despite rules changes designed to encourage their attendance.

Perhaps no change in the rules has been more controversial than affirmative action, which gets to the heart of such matters as theories of equality, compensatory justice, and race relations in the United States. I have no light to shed on the merits or drawbacks of such programs, although it is worth noting that the brutal exclusion of blacks from party affairs in the South is well behind us. More to the point is to consider whether such changes have affected the power balance within the Democratic party.

It is probably no exaggeration to suggest that, for many supporters of George McGovern's candidacy in 1972, affirmative action involved the hidden agenda of bringing more McGovern delegates to Miami Beach. According to Jeane Kirkpatrick's data, two-thirds of the delegates who were younger than age thirty backed McGovern, while less than half the delegates age thirty and over voted for him; and nearly two-thirds of women delegates supported McGovern, while less than half the men delegates did.[21] If this continued to be the pattern at Democratic conventions, then liberal activists can be considered to have scored a real political coup, getting more liberal delegates to the convention under the guise of broadening the delegates' demographic base. But has it continued to be the pattern? According to a CBS News analysis, the answer is no, at least for 1976. That year the supporters of Jimmy Carter, who was widely perceived as less liberal than most of his leading competitors, were slightly *more* likely to be young, black, or female than other delegates were.[22]

If delegates' demographic backgrounds are not correlated with their candidate preferences in any systematic and consistent way, we should wonder about the political significance of the affirmative-action rules. These rules may be important in symbolizing a party's commitment to soliciting support from certain groups and in enabling various activists to attend the convention who otherwise might have been excluded. But it would be difficult to argue that they have had an important impact on the outcomes of conventions. It is similarly difficult to perceive how the increasing disunity within delegations to Democratic conventions may have affected the party's internal power balance. Whether convention outcomes have changed for other reasons is the subject of the next two chapters.

FIVE

Intraparty Factionalism

If party leaders have lost their ability to bargain at national conventions, then we might expect a new kind of factionalism to arise over Presidential nominations.[1] My assumption here is that each state party reflects an underlying political culture, ideology, and demographic base. A California party will naturally differ from a Kansas party, a Rhode Island party, and a Mississippi party on all these dimensions. Left to their own devices, partisans in each of these states will tend to vote with those from other states that share important background characteristics.

In an earlier age, when party leaders were in charge, delegates were not left to their own devices.[2] Each convention, with a new set of candidates and a new strategic environment, produced new bargaining consequences. Party leaders were eager to jump on the winner's bandwagon so they would be favored with patronage if the nominee reached the White House. The boss of Pennsylvania, who at the preceding convention found an alliance with New York expedient, now estimates his best bet to lie with Illinois, while the New Yorkers throw in their lot with their old foe California. These bosses could ride roughshod over potentially stable cleavage patterns in order to shift their allegiance to the winning candidate. A leader in search of an electable ticket and patronage is likely to feel the ties of culture, ideology, and demography grow weaker in his chest as the scent of victory fills his nostrils.

When such leaders lose their control over delegates, little stands in the way of a state's voting again and again for a certain kind of candidate who appeals to that state's cultural, ideological, or demographic profile. Therefore I hypothesize that in recent years there have been stable cleavage patterns over time in both parties—

a *persistence* of factionalism. Because, as I noted in Chapter 1, we have no precise measure of the decline of bossism, all I can do is show that such persistence has arisen; it is not possible to link it to exact moments of organizational decay. Most important for my purpose in this volume, however, is to show not only whether but *when* such persistence began. If it began in 1972, we can infer that the rules broke the back of boss rule; if it began earlier, a longer-term development was occurring. By itself, this finding does not establish when the leaders declined, but it does indicate what a plausible consequence of such a decline would be.

Methodology

The best measure of factionalism is the vote cast at the convention, and I am not the first to compare roll-call votes with each other to discover persistent factionalism or other significant phenomena. Unlike most other scholars, however, I am using the actual vote percentage that a state cast for a candidate or resolution, instead of simply dividing states into two broad groupings and performing Guttman scaling or setting up a four-cell table.[3] This latter procedure lumps together too many delegations of widely differing behavior patterns; for example, a "pro-Mondale" grouping would include delegations that gave him all their votes with those that gave him 51 percent. I prefer to be sensitive to these differences. One serious objection is that these actual vote percentages are sometimes misleading. The Democrats' earlier use of the unit rule, and both parties' use of winner-take-all delegate selection procedures, may produce what appears to be a unanimous state party but is actually a divided party rendered artificially unanimous by its rules. For example, the California delegation that voted unanimously for George McGovern at the 1972 Democratic convention was "representing" a state party that had given McGovern only 43.5 percent of the vote in the primary. I see no way around this, and except for some experimental adjustments in the Democratic vote to be discussed below, I will take these data at face value if only to be able to utilize the data from states where such percentages are truly meaningful.

Another departure from some earlier studies is my practice of weighting each state equally.[4] The theoretical question I am attempting to answer—whether a state voted the same way convention after convention—is irrelevant to the relative sizes of delegations.

One final preliminary point is to reiterate the finding of Table 4.4 that only a minority of the delegates to either party's national convention from 1952 through 1984 had ever attended a prior convention. This suggests that any persistent cleavage patterns I discover are probably not the result of continuity of delegates' attendance. If I establish a continuity of cleavage patterns, it will exist despite high turnover of individual delegates and will be all the more significant a discovery.

The use of the actual percentage a state cast for a candidate or resolution enables us to use factor analysis over time to uncover longitudinal dimensions.[5] Which roll-call votes will be analyzed? I decided to select from each convention only one key vote, since the use of more than one vote from some conventions and not others might produce factors strongly geared toward the multivote years. For each convention, I sought a vote that best approximated the factional division at that convention. This led to the adoption of decision rules based on several assumptions: that the most important business of the convention is nomination, first of the President and second of the Vice-President; that decisions on the platform, credentials, and rules are also important but less so than nominations; and that any of these votes can, at different conventions, best express the factional cleavage at that convention. Therefore I adopted the following decision rules:

1. In a contested convention, the key vote was the nominee's highest vote on the ballot before obvious bandwagon effects set in.[6]
2. If the Presidential nomination was uncontested but the Vice-Presidential nomination was contested, using the same definition, the key vote was the appropriate vote for that nominee.
3. If neither nomination was contested and one roll-call vote was taken on another matter, that was the key vote.
4. If none of the above conditions occurred, and there was more than one non-nominating vote, the key vote was the one that was fairly evenly divided and, according to Richard Bain, highly correlated with whatever little division occurred on the Presidential ballot.[7] This produced the vote on rules at the 1908 Republican convention and the vote on the Texas delegation's credentials at the 1928 Re-

publican convention. At the off-year Democratic conference of 1974, two votes were taken on whether to conduct future off-year meetings; I used the vote on the Banks Amendment because it was more highly correlated with the votes of other conventions of this period than was the other vote, which was correlated with the Banks Amendment with a Pearson's correlation coefficient of .664.

Finally, I should note that several conventions produced no appropriate roll-call votes and are missing from this analysis. They are the Democratic conventions of 1928, 1936, and 1964, and the Republican conventions of 1900, 1936, 1944, 1956, 1960, 1980, and 1984.

Findings

The Democrats

The results of factor-analyzing the Democratic key votes from 1896 through 1984 appear in Table 5.1.[8] In this case, the party-decline thesis appears to be confirmed. Of the seven factors, only the first had high loadings for more than one or two conventions, and it involved all conventions from 1960 through 1980. Therefore, by 1960 the loosening of the reins held by party leaders had occurred to an extent that was sufficient to allow the factional division at that convention to be replicated at every succeeding divided convention.

Two features of Table 5.1 need elaboration, and the first is why some of the high loadings on the crucial first factor are positive while others are negative. Examination of those votes leads us to conclude that there was an underlying dimension that can best be thought of as ideological. The votes whose loadings are positive represent the liberal side at those conventions: Kennedy in 1960 (whose major opponent was the relatively conservative Southerner, Johnson), McGovern in 1972, the pro-reform Banks Amendment in 1974, and opposition to cutting the social services budget in 1978. The votes that have negative loadings were those supporting Humphrey in 1968 and Carter in 1976 and 1980, in which their main opponents were liberals. The first factor in Table 5.1 can therefore be appropriately described as ideological.

The second feature of Table 5.1 that requires comment is the rela-

TABLE 5.1. Varimax rotated factor matrix, Democratic roll-call votes, 1896–1984

	Factor 1	Factor 2	Factor 3	Factor 4	Factor 5	Factor 6	Factor 7
Bryan, 4P, 1896	−.211	−.824	−.029	+.163	−.009	+.040	−.078
Stevenson, 1VP, 1900	+.005	−.008	−.003	+.030	−.048	+.064	+.751
Parker, 1P, 1904	−.257	+.122	+.574	−.101	−.153	−.002	+.107
Pa. Cred., 1908	+.072	+.072	+.133	−.389	+.234	−.174	−.133
Wilson, 40P, 1912	+.176	−.044	+.132	+.331	+.140	+.459	−.012
Women Suff., 1916	−.107	+.115	+.592	−.094	+.051	−.061	−.144
Cox, 43P, 1920	+.003	+.034	+.088	−.049	+.044	−.880	−.060
Davis, 102P, 1924	−.398	−.125	+.567	−.132	−.017	+.376	+.248
Roosevelt, 3P, 1932	−.227	−.407	−.261	+.327	−.092	+.247	−.070
Wallace, 1VP, 1940	+.334	+.326	−.020	+.596	+.194	−.111	+.155
Truman, 2VP, 1944	−.008	+.097	+.100	−.572	−.008	−.057	+.043
Truman, 1P, 1948	+.652	+.151	−.319	+.159	+.280	+.101	−.037
Stevenson, 2P, 1952	+.089	+.153	−.105	+.042	+.968	+.014	+.103
Stevenson, 1P, 1956	+.387	−.040	−.025	+.446	+.310	+.091	−.295
Kennedy, 1P, 1960	+.698	+.045	−.008	+.257	+.175	+.047	+.128
Humphrey, 1P, 1968	−.477	+.243	+.221	−.186	+.302	+.211	−.137
McGovern, 1P, 1972	+.694	−.022	−.307	−.014	+.026	−.178	+.252
Banks Amend., 1974	+.543	−.054	−.340	−.155	+.004	+.087	+.077
Carter, 1P, 1976	−.543	+.422	+.210	+.031	+.192	+.165	+.049
Budget Res., 1978	+.621	−.077	+.045	−.036	−.101	+.128	−.252
Carter, 1P, 1980	−.834	−.265	+.138	−.078	−.155	+.009	+.141
Mondale, 1P, 1984	−.267	+.545	+.104	+.116	+.137	−.034	−.155
Eigenvalue	4.855	2.220	1.790	1.119	1.031	.897	.724
% Variance	38.4	17.6	14.2	8.9	8.2	7.1	5.7

Note: Number and letters after candidate's name refer to the number of the ballot and the office contested.

tively low loading of the Mondale vote in 1984. Did the era of factional continuity end in 1980, and are the Democrats back in a period of random voting alignments? Alternatively, have the Democrats entered a new era of stable alignments, different from the 1960–1980 period? I believe that the answer is neither, because the vote for Gary Hart in 1984, when substituted for the Mondale vote, has a respectably high (and positive) loading on the first factor. It seems apparent that Hart's support came from the normal liberal Democratic base. This supposition is made plausible by Hart's deliberate use of Kennedy-style rhetoric and gestures, his background in the 1972 McGovern campaign, and his endorsements from some key Kennedy allies such as Theodore Sorensen and Abraham Ribicoff; compare this with Mondale's ties with Humphrey and Carter. However, Mondale was deprived of his natural base by the candidacy of Jesse Jackson, whose five best state delegations were in the South. Had Jackson not cut into Mondale's strength, the Minnesotan would have enjoyed the whole conservative base. Public opinion surveys at the time indeed showed that Jackson was hurting Mondale, not Hart.

Was the 1984 convention part of the new factional alignment in the Democratic party? The answer is yes, if we combine the Mondale and Jackson votes. Doing so, however, would violate the criteria outlined earlier for choosing convention votes. If we combine the Mondale and Jackson votes, then why not play a similar game with other conventions? Soon the reader would lose confidence in the objectivity of the exercise and wonder whether I had been "cooking the data." There is another reason not to tamper with Table 5.1. If the first factor is ideological, it would stretch credulity to assign Jesse Jackson and his "rainbow coalition" to the conservative side of the contest in 1984. Clearly Jackson's appeal was primarily racial, and a disproportionate number of blacks live in the most conservative of Democratic states in the South. Therefore an unusually left-wing Democrat received his strongest support from areas that normally back the most right-wing candidates. I shall refrain from compounding this confusion by putting Jackson in a conservative coalition.

How did the states fall along the 1960–1980 dimension? Answering this question required giving each state a score, and I decided not to use factor scores because they would involve the use of data from earlier conventions that were not truly part of this di-

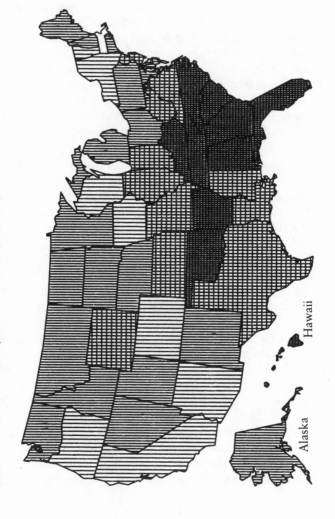

FIGURE 5.1. Standardized factional score, Democratic conventions, 1960–1980

SAS/GRAPH

LEGEND: SCORE

LESS THAN −2
0 TO −1
MORE THAN +1

−1 TO −2
0 TO +1

Hawaii

Alaska

mension. Instead, I created a standardized measure of the votes from 1960 through 1980 by (1) creating a standardized score on each vote for each state, (2) adding the scores for all the conventions together for each state, and (3) standardizing the result. This produces a measure indicating how far from the convention mean each state stood on the dimension. In each case, I manipulated the signs so that a positive sign indicated a conservative vote, a negative sign a liberal vote.

As Figure 5.1 demonstrates, the resulting geographic patterns are striking. Every Southern and border state except Maryland is more conservative than the national mean, as are several Northern states, including Illinois, Indiana, and New Jersey. When we take into account that Ohio and Pennsylvania fall to the liberal side by less than .03 standard deviations each, we can see an unbroken belt of relatively conservative non-Southern industrial states from Missouri to New Jersey. Most of the rest of the North is on the liberal side, but the most liberal states are clustered in three regions: the Northeast (Massachusetts, New York, and Vermont), the upper Midwest (Iowa and Wisconsin), and the Far West (Arizona, California, Colorado, and Oregon). Two observations suggest that political culture may be an important correlate of this dimension. One is that the belt from Missouri to New Jersey, noted above, includes a group of states long noted for the prevalence of machine politics. The other is that the very liberal states of the Midwest and the Far West tend to be those with a long Progressive, antimachine tradition—notably California, Oregon, and Wisconsin. We are seeing not only North versus South but also machine professionals versus amateur reformers, the intraparty cleavage first analyzed by James Q. Wilson.[9]

The most sweeping attempt at a taxonomic scheme based on cultural variables has been that of Daniel Elazar.[10] As described in Chapter 4, Elazar describes three cultures: the "individualistic," based on a politics of material incentives closely resembling machine politics; the "moralistic," based on issues and ideologies and suggestive of amateur reformers; and the "traditionalistic," based on deference and located primarily in the South. Moreover, Elazar has identified each state's dominant and secondary cultures. The Z-scores described above appear in Table 5.2, grouped by Elazar's categories and subcategories. Note that all but two of the traditionalistic states are more conservative than the mean and that all

TABLE 5.2. Standardized scores on factor, Democratic national conventions, 1960–1980, by Elazar's political culture categories

Dominant and Secondary Cultures	State	Score
Traditionalistic	Alabama	+1.06
	Arkansas	+1.50
	Georgia	+1.18
	Louisiana	+0.90
	Mississippi	+0.86
	South Carolina	+1.73
	Tennessee	+1.71
	Virginia	+0.81
Traditionalistic	Florida	+1.31
(Individualistic)	Kentucky	+1.41
	New Mexico	−0.24
	Oklahoma	+1.03
	Texas	+0.84
	West Virginia	+0.16
Traditionalistic	Arizona	−1.59
(Moralistic)	Hawaii	+1.24
	North Carolina	+1.53
Individualistic (Traditionalistic)	Missouri	+0.86
Individualistic	Alaska	−0.36
	Delaware	+0.34
	Illinois	+0.83
	Indiana	+0.07
	Maryland	−0.13
	Nevada	−0.22
	New Jersey	+0.48
	Ohio	−0.02
	Pennsylvania	−0.02
Individualistic	Connecticut	−0.40
(Moralistic)	Massachusetts	−2.03
	Nebraska	−0.50
	New York	−1.08
	Rhode Island	−0.98

TABLE 5.2. (continued)

Dominant and Secondary Cultures	State	Score
	Wyoming	+0.53
Moralistic	California	−1.71
(Individualistic)	Idaho	−0.13
	Iowa	−1.07
	Kansas	+0.22
	Montana	−0.29
	New Hampshire	−0.92
	South Dakota	−0.80
	Washington	−0.14
Moralistic	Colorado	−1.04
	Maine	−0.76
	Michigan	−0.55
	Minnesota	−0.19
	North Dakota	−0.42
	Oregon	−1.29
	Utah	−0.61
	Vermont	−1.68
	Wisconsin	−1.52
Group means:		
Traditionalistic		+0.91
Individualistic		+0.09
Moralistic		−0.76

but one of the moralistic states are more liberal than the mean. The individualistic states fall in between, with about half on each side of the mean. The end of the table shows that the traditionalistic states are well to the conservative side, the moralistic states nearly as far to the left, and the individualistic states straddle the center. Moreover, if we assign each cluster of states in Table 5.2 a score based on the cluster's rank order from the purely traditionalistic to the purely moralistic, the score correlates with the Z-score with a Pearson's coefficient of .726.

The reader might suspect that the trend I have discovered may be the result of termination of the unit rule at the 1968 Democratic convention. In order to test for this possibility, I took the states that had the unit rule in 1956[11] and changed their 1960-to-1980 votes as though they still had the unit rule; then I performed the factor analysis summarized in Table 5.1, with virtually the same results as in that table. The same thing occurred when I ran the factor analysis with the unit-rule states excluded.

As expected, only in recent years has there been a stable cleavage pattern at Democratic national conventions, and that pattern antedated the McGovern-Fraser reforms. I suspect that the factions associated with the pattern are correlated with their states' political cultures because so many recent conventions have involved clashes over reforms in party rules and "style" issues that go beyond traditional class cleavages. These issues include foreign policy, feminism, abortion, homosexual rights, and affirmative action. But it is beyond my scope here to give a full accounting of this pattern;[12] for my purposes, it is sufficient to show that this persistence arose and that it arose long before 1972.

The Republicans

The results of factor-analyzing the Republican votes from 1896 through 1976 appear in Table 5.3. Here again my hypothesis is handsomely confirmed, with only the first factor having high loadings on several conventions, all of them the most recent. Indeed, we can see the dimension begin to emerge in 1948 and steadily increase the loadings until the acme in 1972, the only vote on a resolution and therefore not affected directly by candidate considerations. These data belie the arguments of those who, like Gerald Pomper, see the Ford-Reagan cleavage pattern in 1976 as unique.[13] Here again the underlying dimension seems to be ideological. Conservatives Goldwater and Nixon and the apportionment formula favored by the right in 1972 have positive loadings, while the relatively liberal Ford has a negative loading.

Again I gave each state a standardized score on this factor, using only the conventions from 1964 through 1976. I divided the period at 1964 because the jump in the absolute value of the loadings was greatest from 1952 to 1964; omitting 1952 also enabled me to include Alaska and Hawaii, as throughout this analysis I have been excluding nonstate areas.[14] Here the geographic configuration shown in Figure 5.2 is clear. Conservative strength is in the South-

TABLE 5.3. Varimax rotated factor matrix, Republican roll-call votes, 1896–1976

	Factor 1	Factor 2	Factor 3	Factor 4	Factor 5	Factor 6
Hobart, 1VP, 1896	−.027	+.057	−.038	+.084	+.038	−.471
Hawaii Amend., 1904	−.060	−.055	−.014	+.061	+.819	−.094
Rules Report, 1908	+.235	+.070	+.715	−.085	−.277	+.157
Taft, 1P, 1912	+.258	+.282	+.038	+.387	−.115	+.514
Hughes, 2P, 1916	−.069	+.508	+.103	+.340	+.245	−.034
Harding, 9P, 1920	+.011	−.190	+.537	+.282	+.076	+.394
Dawes, 3VP, 1924	−.049	+.155	+.021	+.066	+.384	−.022
Texas Cred., 1928	−.019	−.984	+.025	+.054	−.023	+.044
Curtis, 1VP, 1932	+.123	+.075	+.531	−.136	+.188	−.129
Willkie, 5P, 1940	−.070	−.132	−.125	+.488	+.314	+.028
Dewey, 1P, 1948	+.259	+.080	+.096	+.345	+.280	−.342
Eisenhower, 1P, 1952	−.343	+.237	−.108	+.689	−.013	−.148
Goldwater, 1P, 1964	+.499	−.119	+.438	−.400	−.024	+.454
Nixon, 1P, 1968	+.610	−.043	+.022	−.020	+.031	−.020
Apport. Amend., 1972	+.911	−.012	+.235	−.108	−.167	+.055
Ford, 1P, 1976	−.525	−.186	−.270	+.167	+.217	−.309
Eigenvalue	3.445	1.733	1.256	1.061	.788	.576
% Variance	38.9	19.6	14.2	12.0	8.9	6.5

Note: Number and letters after candidate's name refer to the number of the ballot and the office contested.

FIGURE 5.2. Standardized factional score, Republican conventions, 1964–1976

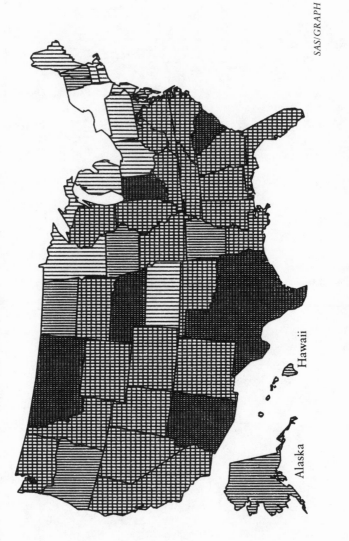

Alaska

Hawaii

SAS/GRAPH

LEGEND: SCORE

	LESS THAN -2		-1 TO -2
	0 TO -1		0 TO +1
	MORE THAN +1		

east and the Far West (excluding Alaska and Hawaii, reserved for a special category in Table 5.4), liberal strength is in the Northeast and parts of the Midwest. The Northeast is by far the most liberal region, while the continental Far West is only slightly less conservative than the Southeast.

Why have the Southeast and the Far West been the heartland of recent Republican conservatism? Perhaps the increase in salience of certain issues—race, with its special significance for the South, and military issues, with the high concentration of defense and space industries in the so-called Sunbelt—since 1952 helps to explain a new breed of Republican conservatism.[15] Moreover, this new breed has clearly arisen where the party has made relative gains. If we plot the long-term rise or decline in the standardized Republican Presidential vote percentage from 1932 to 1976, we can assign each state a slope based on the linear trend. The correlation between this slope and the Z-scores of Table 5.4 is .672, with the states with the highest Republican gains being most conservative. Nor is this simply a result of the fact that the South saw the greatest Republican gains; with the former Confederate states removed, the correlation increases to .763, reflecting the fact that higher-than-average Republican gains occurred in the Far West as well. This implies that this new kind of conservatism, so uncorrelated with the Taft conservatism of the 1940s and early 1950s, was a phenomenon arising when "new men" took over moribund party machinery.

As with the Democrats, these speculations are not central to my argument. What is central is that beginning in 1964 an unprecedentedly stable alignment arose in Republican convention politics.

The Balance of Power

Now that ideological factions within each party have been identified, we can assign each state an ideological score based on the mean percentage for the conservative side at each of the conventions in the 1960–1980 period. This will enable us to determine which side is dominant in each party, how the balance of power may be shifting, and how delegation apportionment formulas may affect that balance.

TABLE 5.4. Standardized scores on factor, Republican national conventions, 1964–1976, by region

Region	State	Score	Regional mean
Northeast	Connecticut	−1.74	
	Delaware	−0.10	
	Maine	−1.33	
	Maryland	−0.73	
	Massachusetts	−1.70	
	New Hampshire	−0.35	
	New Jersey	−1.27	
	New York	−2.02	
	Pennsylvania	−1.75	
	Rhode Island	−2.04	
	Vermont	−0.70	
	West Virginia	+0.15	−1.13
Southeast	Alabama	+0.86	
	Arkansas	−0.17	
	Florida	+0.59	
	Georgia	+0.94	
	Kentucky	+0.58	
	Louisiana	+0.93	
	Mississippi	+0.80	
	North Carolina	+0.28	
	South Carolina	+1.05	
	Tennessee	+0.84	
	Texas	+1.04	
	Virginia	+0.90	+0.72
Midwest	Illinois	+0.24	
	Indiana	+1.13	
	Iowa	−0.44	
	Kansas	−1.18	
	Michigan	−1.67	
	Minnesota	−1.30	
	Missouri	+0.45	
	Nebraska	+1.03	
	North Dakota	−0.03	

TABLE 5.4. (continued)

Region	State	Score	Regional mean
	Ohio	−1.24	
	Oklahoma	+0.95	
	South Dakota	+0.76	
	Wisconsin	+0.05	−0.10
Far West	Arizona	+1.22	
	California	+0.38	
	Colorado	+0.79	
	Idaho	+0.78	
	Montana	+1.09	
	Nevada	+0.80	
	New Mexico	+0.83	
	Oregon	−0.38	
	Utah	+0.60	
	Washington	+0.50	
	Wyoming	+0.91	+0.68
Pacific	Alaska	−0.45	
	Hawaii	−0.91	−0.68

There are several ways to measure the power balance. The most straightforward is simply to view the vote totals on each key ballot. However, short-term factors always influence how states vote on particular matters—a normally liberal state might support a conservative favorite son, a rules battle (such as the Republicans' in 1972) might affect a state's interests apart from its ideological leanings. Another method, less susceptible to short-term influences, would make use of the ideological score described in the previous paragraph. For each year, we can take those states whose mean vote was more than 50 percent conservative and see what proportion of the total vote was cast by these states. This enables us to ascertain secular trends. Finally, we can derive an "expected" conservative vote for each year by multiplying each state's conservative percentage by the number of votes it cast and summing the results.

In the absence of short-term factors, the result should give us the conservative total vote for the convention.[16]

The Democrats

Which side has been winning at Democratic conventions since 1960? Table 5.5 shows that the conservatives won five out of seven times, with a mean vote percentage of 58.7 for the conservative side. The two liberal victories were by relatively narrow margins, and the most recent liberal victory was the McGovern nomination of 1972.

What has the trend been? In Table 5.6, I have grouped the states by their ideological mean, and it is clear that conservatives have outnumbered liberals. States that usually vote conservative outnumbered liberal states in their voting strength by a margin of two to one in the early 1960s and about five to three more recently. The expected vote has been in the high 50 to 60 percent range. But note that there was a gradual trend in the liberal direction until 1980, when Carter's electoral strength in the South was reflected in an

TABLE 5.5. Outcome of key votes, Democratic national conventions, 1960–1980

Vote	Conservative position	Liberal position
1960: Presidential nomination	Others 47.0%	Kennedy 53.0%
1968: Presidential nomination	Humphrey 67.1%	Others 32.9%
1972: Presidential nomination	Others 42.7%	McGovern 57.3%
1974: Banks amendment	Against 55.0%	For 45.0%
1976: Presidential nomination	Carter 74.4%	Others 25.6%
1978: Budget resolution	Against 61.2%	For 38.8%
1980: Presidential nomination	Carter 63.7%	Others 36.3%

TABLE 5.6. Factional strength at Democratic national conventions, 1960–1984, based on mean support of each state for conservative side of key votes (nonstate areas excluded)

Mean conservative support	1960	1964	1968	1972	1976	1980	1984	Electoral votes	
								1972–1980	1984–1988
75–100%	30.7%	29.3%	27.2%	25.8%	25.4%	27.3%	30.3%	30.5%	31.8%
50–74.9%	35.9	36.8	36.6	36.2	36.1	35.1	33.9	34.0	33.1
Total conservative	66.6	66.1	63.8	62.0	61.5	62.4	64.2	64.5	64.9
25–49.9%	30.7	30.9	33.4	34.5	35.0	34.2	32.8	32.9	32.7
0–24.9%	2.7	3.0	2.8	3.4	3.5	3.4	3.0	2.6	2.4
Total liberal	33.4	33.9	36.2	38.0	38.5	37.6	35.8	35.5	35.1
Expected conservative vote	60.3	59.8	58.8	57.8	57.5	58.1	59.3	59.5	59.9

upsurge in that region's delegate apportionment. The conservative trend continued into 1984.

I have also included electoral vote analyses in Table 5.6 in order to show what the result would have been if the party had distributed delegates according to electoral college strength alone. The fact that the conservatives' expected vote is usually lower than their electoral vote strength makes it clear that the Democrats' apportionment formula has benefited the liberals in recent years. At their most recent conventions, the Democrats have used a formula based equally on electoral college strength and on the popular vote for recent Democratic Presidential nominees. This helps the liberals in two ways.

First, the formula aids large states by paying attention to the size of the popular vote. The ten largest states in 1970, with approximately 48 percent of the electoral vote in the 1970s (excluding the District of Columbia), cast about 54 percent of the vote at the next three Democratic conventions. Moreover, large states tend to vote Democratic in Presidential elections: In the three most recent close elections of 1960, 1968, and 1976, the mean state carried by the Democrats had 13.5, 13.6, and 12.4 electoral votes respectively, while the figures for states carried by the Republicans were 8.5, 9.4, and 8.9. In the Democratic party, these ten large states are slightly more liberal than the rest, casting a mean of 56.5 percent for the conservative side while the mean for the other forty states was 61.4 percent. Therefore, by favoring large states the Democrats favor liberal states.

A second reason the formula helps liberals is that it concentrates on voting in Presidential elections. Southern states tend to be Democratic in state and local elections and often vote for Republican or third-party candidates for the White House. This means that when an Eisenhower, a Goldwater, a Nixon, a Wallace, or a Reagan runs well in the South, these conservative states lose votes at the subsequent Democratic national convention. Table 5.6 also shows that the 1980 Census resulted in an almost negligible gain for the liberal states at Democratic national conventions.

The Republicans

In order to assess factional strength at recent Republican conventions, I am going to make one modification in the key votes listed in Table 5.3. In 1968, as the table indicates, Richard Nixon's coalition was essentially conservative, but we would be remiss in treating it as the sum and substance of Republican conservatism at that convention were we to ignore Ronald Reagan, who received about 14 percent of the vote. The conservative faction at that convention is most appropriately measured by adding together the Nixon and Reagan votes. While Nixon did receive some support from party moderates and liberals, such as Senator Hatfield and Governor Volpe, his most powerful allies were Senators Goldwater, Thurmond, and Tower. As Table 5.7 shows, combining the Nixon and Reagan votes gives the conservatives the same roughly two-thirds of the vote that they received in 1964 and 1972.

The table also shows what is familiar to observers of recent Republican politics: since 1964, conservatives have almost invariably controlled Republican conventions by a heavy margin. Even the exception of 1976 was indicative of conservative strength. Gerald Ford ran a relatively conservative administration, and there were few differences between him and Reagan on the platform.[17] He was supported at the convention by many conservatives, including the aforementioned trio of Goldwater, Thurmond and Tower, and according to the University of Michigan Survey Research Center and Center for Political Studies survey, Republicans who voted for Ford in the primaries were even more likely than Republican Reagan voters to call themselves conservatives. Yet even this conservative

TABLE 5.7. Outcome of key votes, Republican national conventions, 1964–1976

Vote	Conservative position	Liberal position
1964: Presidential nomination	Goldwater 67.5%	Others 32.5%
1968: Presidential nomination	Nixon or Reagan 65.6%	Others 34.4%
1972: Minority rules report	Against 67.6%	For 32.4%
1976: Presidential nomination	Reagan 47.4%	Ford 52.5%

incumbent nearly lost his nomination to the ideologically "purer" Reagan, illustrating the power of Republican conservatives. And Reagan won the nomination all but unanimously four years later.

What has been the trend in conservative strength? Table 5.8 is similar to Table 5.6 for the Democrats, and it shows that the conservatives have had about the same majority in the Republican party as they did among the Democrats, but with one difference: the trend is more consistently toward the right. By 1984 more than half the votes at Republican conventions were cast by the most conservative group. Moreover, as the electoral vote data imply, the apportionment formula has favored the conservative states: (1) Most delegate votes are based on electoral votes, which are slightly weighted toward small states, (2) states get the same number of bonus votes regardless of their size, and (3) small states by and large tend to vote Republican, as noted above, and thus win more bonus votes. The ten largest states in 1970, with approximately 48 percent of the electoral votes in the 1970s (excluding the District of Columbia), cast about 44 percent of the votes at the next three Republican conventions. When this is combined with the fact that large states tend to vote liberal at Republican conventions—the ten largest states cast an average of 46 percent for the conservative side of these key votes, compared with a mean of 72 percent for the rest of the states—it is clear that the apportionment formula aids the right. The 1980 Census aided conservative states even more. While a Ford can be nominated under certain circumstances, it would appear that the right wing is increasing its hold on the Republican party. As Clarke Reed, the conservative chairman of the Mississippi Republican party, has put it, "There's no ideological contest in the party anymore. We've won that." [18]

Conclusions

I have demonstrated that a persistent factional alignment arose in the early 1960s in both major parties, an alignment that continues to the present day. While interpretation of this fact may vary, I have attributed it to the decline of party leaders who could treat delegates as pawns. If members of the 1972 school accept that this persistence is symptomatic of the decline of state and local lead-

TABLE 5.8. Factional strength at Republican national conventions, 1960–1984, based on mean support of each state for conservative side of key votes (nonstate areas excluded)

Mean conservative support	1960	1964	1968	1972	1976	1980	1984	Electoral votes 1972–1980	Electoral votes 1984–1988
75–100%	46.0%	47.8%	48.3%	49.2%	49.8%	49.9%	52.4%	49.3%	51.8%
50–74.9%	18.2	17.7	16.9	17.5	16.9	17.4	16.6	15.5	15.3
Total conservative	64.2	65.5	65.2	66.7	66.6	67.4	69.0	64.9	67.1
25–49.9%	14.1	13.8	14.4	13.7	13.7	13.3	12.2	13.6	13.1
0–24.9%	21.7	20.8	20.4	19.6	19.7	19.3	18.7	21.5	19.8
Total liberal	35.8	34.5	34.8	33.3	33.4	32.6	31.0	35.1	32.9
Expected conservative vote	60.5	61.5	61.9	62.7	62.9	63.3	64.5	62.0	63.7

ers, they will have to explain why the trend first arose before the McGovern-Fraser reforms were implemented.

In a departure from the main argument here, I have also demonstrated that the conservative faction within each party generally wins, and in both parties that faction has been slowly gaining in strength. I should end with a cautionary note that we not exaggerate the degree of factional persistence revealed here. A useful concept here is V. O. Key's "dualism in a moving consensus,"[19] which can be applied to this phenomenon by noting that although we can speak of a great deal of consistency as to which states were more liberal than others, the issues over which they conflict change over time. The Southern delegations that opposed John F. Kennedy in 1960 included many who favored racial segregation; in 1976 and 1980 those same states backed the relatively conservative Jimmy Carter, who like many of his fellow white Southerners had come to accept the civil rights gains of the 1950s and 1960s. On the Republican side, we can see a transition from Barry Goldwater in 1964, who sought to overturn the legacy of the New Deal, to Ronald Reagan in 1980, who paid lip service to that tradition by quoting approvingly in his acceptance speech a speech of Franklin D. Roosevelt's. The issues and emphases change, but the states line up the same way.

SIX

Who Is Nominated?

Ultimately a system such as the Presidential nominating process must be judged by the nature of its outcomes, and it has been alleged that the characteristics of nominees have changed. Some of these changes will not be hard to document, but as in earlier chapters the essential question will be the timing of such trends. I shall examine several characteristics of nominees—their demographic backgrounds, the extent to which they have run an ideological campaign, and the public offices they have held—and finally, I shall look at Vice-Presidential nominations.

The Death of "Availability"

When party leaders controlled the system, they were often able to veto the nominations of certain kinds of candidates who did not fit the prevailing standards of "availability." In the late 1950s, in a tongue-in-cheek but reasonably accurate description, Clinton Rossiter spelled out these criteria for the nominee:

He must be, according to unwritten law: a man, a white, a Christian.

He almost certainly must be: a Northerner or Westerner, less than sixty-five years old, of Northern European stock, experienced in politics and public service, healthy.

He ought to be: from a state larger than Kentucky, more than forty-five years old, a family man, of British stock, a veteran, a Protestant, a lawyer, a state governor, a Mason, Legionnaire, or Rotarian—preferably all three, a small-town boy, a self-made man, especially if a Republican, experienced in international affairs, a cultural middle-brow who likes baseball, detective stories, fishing, pop concerts, picnics, and seascapes.

It really makes no difference whether he is: a college graduate, a small businessman, a member of Congress, a member of the Cabinet, a defeated candidate for the Presidency, providing that he emerged from his defeat the very image of the happy warrior.

He ought not to be: from a state smaller than Kentucky, divorced, a bachelor, a Catholic, a former Catholic, a corporation president, a twice-defeated candidate for the Presidency, an intellectual, even if blooded in the political wars, a professional soldier, a professional politician, conspicuously rich.

He almost certainly cannot be: a Southerner . . . , of Polish, Italian, or Slavic stock, a union official, an ordained minister.

He cannot be, according to unwritten law: a Negro, a Jew, an Oriental, a woman, an atheist, a freak.[1]

Times have changed. First came John Kennedy—under forty-five, Irish, Roman Catholic, "conspicuously rich." Then came Barry Goldwater—of Polish-Jewish descent and from one of the nation's smallest states. Eight years after that came George McGovern, another small-stater, and after him came Jimmy Carter, from the heart of Dixie. Most recently we have Ronald Reagan, a divorced senior citizen whose former career would surely have been included in Rossiter's list of disqualifications had he imagined that any movie actor would have been seriously considered for the White House. None of the nominees from 1960 through 1972 were governors, and since 1960 only three of the ten men nominated were lawyers: Nixon, Ford, and Mondale.

And these were just the nominees. Among the serious contenders were small-staters Frank Church, Robert Dole, Fred Harris, Edmund Muskie, Morris Udall, and Gary Hart; bachelor Jerry Brown; the divorced Dole and Nelson Rockefeller; Southerners Howard Baker, George Bush, John Connally, and George Wallace; Irish-Catholics Brown, Robert and Edward Kennedy, and Eugene McCarthy; Polish-Catholic Muskie; and of course Jesse Jackson. And surely Greek-American Spiro Agnew would have been a serious contender in 1976 had the law not intervened. Indeed, it is remarkable how quickly the old taboos fall. After 1960, no candidate's Catholicism has been held against him or scarcely even noticed (except for Jerry Brown's seminary training), and four years after all the attention given to Carter's roots, three Southern Republicans entered the fray with scant attention paid to their regional peculiarity.

Like most observers of these trends, I interpret them as the result of the inability of party leaders to exercise the veto I described above. If this is so, then that veto was dying long before the McGovern-Fraser reforms. We can find earlier examples of violations of availability criteria—William Jennings Bryan from a small state, Irish-Catholic Alfred Smith, the divorced Adlai Stevenson—but there clearly seems to be a plethora of latter-day exceptions to the old rules.

Relying as I do on quantitative evidence whenever possible, I shall examine the trend in one specific quantifiable area: the size of the nominee's state. Since the number and distribution of electoral votes have varied over the years, I have converted each state's votes to normalized scores and present those of the home states of nominees and other major candidates in Table 6.1. Here I make no distinction between contested and uncontested conventions, because it is useful to see whether even consensual nominees come from large or small states.

The results for the Democrats confirm the party-decline thesis. Before 1960 the only small-state nominee was William Jennings Bryan, and the only other nominees with Z-scores under +1 were Woodrow Wilson and the incumbent Harry Truman. Of the seven nominees from 1960 through 1984, only the incumbent Lyndon Johnson was from a large state. The same trend appears for the losers. There is no similar trend for the Republicans, as Barry Goldwater was the only small-state nominee or major candidate in recent years. There are two possible explanations for this: either Republicans are still looking for large-state nominees or the trend toward small-state candidates was forestalled by the persistent ambitions of several large-state candidates—Richard Nixon, Nelson Rockefeller, and Ronald Reagan. (Among them, they comprised eight of the eleven major candidates from 1960 through 1984.) This is an impossible question to answer, but it is worth noting in defense of the latter explanation that the Presidential ambitions of Spiro Agnew, Howard Baker, Robert Dole, and Lowell Weicker were interrupted by factors other than the modest number of electoral votes of their home states.

TABLE 6.1. Standardized electoral votes of home states of nominees and other major candidates, 1896–1984

Year	Democratic			Republican		
	Nominee	Others	Mean	Nominee	Others	Mean
1896	−0.26	+1.99	+1.24	+1.79	—	+1.79
1900	−0.26	—	−0.26	+1.79	—	+1.79
1904	+3.70	+3.70	+3.70	+3.70	—	+3.70
1908	−0.32	—	−0.32	+1.61	—	+1.61
1912	+0.34	+0.81	+0.69	+1.52	+3.98	+2.75
1916	+0.34	—	+0.34	+3.98	+2.40	+2.93
1920	+1.52	+1.69	+1.63	+1.52	+1.48	+1.49
1924	+3.98	+0.70	+1.17	+0.81	—	+0.81
1928	+3.98	—	+3.98	+0.23	—	+0.23
1932	+4.04	+4.04	+4.04	+1.23	—	+1.23
1936	+4.04	—	+4.04	−0.23	—	−0.23
1940	+4.04	—	+4.04	+4.04	+2.86	+3.25
1944	+4.08	—	+4.08	+4.08	—	+4.08
1948	+0.45	+0.11	+0.28	+4.08	+0.79	+1.89
1952	+1.82	+1.32	+1.45	+3.87	+1.59	+2.73
1956	+1.82	+3.87	+2.85	+2.39	—	+2.39
1960	+0.60	+1.52	+1.06	+2.43	—	+2.43
1964	+1.61	—	+1.61	−0.62	+2.06	+0.72
1968	−0.06	−0.06	−0.06	+3.62	+3.45	+3.51
1972	−0.72	−0.17	−0.35	+3.76	—	+3.76
1976	+0.16	−0.50	−0.17	+1.14	+3.76	+2.45
1980	+0.16	+0.38	+0.27	+3.76	—	+3.76
1984	−0.06	+0.61	+0.39	+4.10		+4.10

The Rise of Ideology

Perhaps even more important than the changes in the demographic background of our Presidential nominees has been the increased propensity for candidates of a marked ideological persuasion to be nominated. Surely the McGovern and Reagan candidacies, as well as the earlier movements behind Goldwater and McCarthy, indicate that ideology has had a major role to play in recent nominations. The evidence in the previous chapter that factional alignments have become more persistent in recent years in both parties is a more than anecdotal indication of the new significance of ongoing issue-based alignments.

Numerous observers argue that the new rules promote the participation of issue-motivated activists—variously called "amateurs" or "purists"—and hence increase the likelihood of an ideological nominee.[2] However, several of them acknowledge that the Goldwater and McCarthy examples indicate that these activists began to become more prominent *before* the rules changes, and even that the activists caused the changes in the rules.[3] In other words, the activists changed the rules in order to increase their strength in the party.

How can we measure the impact of the ideologues? One way is to label various candidates "liberal," "moderate," or "conservative" and then assess the size of each faction by the use of Gallup polls through the primary season. By then looking at how many votes each faction received in the primaries and, most important, at the convention, we can infer how successfully each faction mobilized its forces. Of course, the primary showings are difficult to interpret, since not all states hold primaries, and a candidate might have benefited not from superior mobilization but from the fact that the primary states (not always a representative cross-section of states) were especially receptive to that type of candidate. Primary showings are also influenced by who was on the ballot where.

Moreover, since poll results and primary results influence each other, it is a bit artificial for me to consider them separately. It would be unwise, for example, to regard the survey results as in some way antecedent to the primary results. The reader might wonder why I did not look only at the polls taken before the first primary, and the answer is that such surveys have been notoriously unrelated to the eventual convention showdown, as the experiences of Hubert Humphrey in 1968, George McGovern in 1972, and Jimmy Carter in 1976 demonstrate. Therefore, using polls that were coincident with the primaries provides a sense of public opinion as the race was developing, even if the meaning of such polls is limited.

Nevertheless, if the rules did promote ideological activism, we should expect an improvement in the activating capacities of liberal Democrats and conservative Republicans at conventions beginning in 1972. Because the empirical evidence seems to point in a different direction in each party, I shall consider each one separately.

The Democrats

Because of the increased accuracy of the post-1948 Gallup polls, I shall begin with 1952. In that year, the most liberal names mentioned were those of Estes Kefauver, Averell Harriman, and Paul Douglas.[4] On the right were Richard Russell and Harry Byrd, and in the center were the others, including the nominee, Adlai Stevenson. In Table 6.2 it is apparent that although the liberals (especially Kefauver) ran especially well in the primaries, at the convention they received fewer votes on the first ballot than their strength in the polls merited. Russell and the moderates ran especially well at the convention, Russell because of strong regional support.

Ideological differences among the candidates were muted in 1956, but in 1960 Stevenson and Hubert Humphrey were clearly the favorites of the party's liberal wing,[5] and Lyndon Johnson, George Smathers, and Ross Barnett were the heroes of Southern conservatives. The nominee, John Kennedy, and the others were identified as moderate liberals that year. As Table 6.2 shows, the pattern in 1960 was similar to that of 1952, with liberals underrepresented among the delegates and moderates and conservatives overrepresented.

The 1964 convention was uncontested, and in 1968 Johnson's withdrawal, Robert Kennedy's assassination and Humphrey's abstention from the primaries make analysis difficult. Liberal Eugene McCarthy, the only serious candidate to remain in the race all the way through, received about 35 percent in the polls, 43 percent in the primaries, and 23 percent at the convention—another duplication of the Kefauver pattern.

In 1972 came a major change from earlier years. The liberals— George McGovern, John Lindsay, Shirley Chisholm, and McCarthy—were opposed at the opposite end of the spectrum by George Wallace, Sam Yorty, and Wilbur Mills. Table 6.2 shows the liberals vastly overrepresented at the convention and the other groups underrepresented. Again, conservatives were less underrepresented than moderates. In June the Gallup pollsters asked Democrats to choose between McGovern and Humphrey, and McGovern won by

TABLE 6.2. Showings of Democratic ideological factions in Gallup surveys, primaries, and first-ballot convention votes, selected years, 1952–1980

		Gallup (%)	Primaries (%)	Convention (%)
1952:	Liberals	49	66	38
	Moderates	35 [a]	26	40
	Conservatives	9	8	22
	Don't know	7	0	0
		100	100	100
1960:	Liberals	29	11	8
	Moderates	53	83	62
	Conservatives	12	6	30
	Don't know	6	0	0
		100	100	100
1972:	Liberals	27	33	62
	Moderates	47	43	24
	Conservatives	22	24	14
	Don't know	4	0	0
		100	100	100
1976:	Liberals	15	30	20
	Moderates	68	58	78
	Conservatives	12	12	2
	Don't know	5	0	0
		100	100	100
1980:	Liberals	31	42	35
	Moderates and Conservatives	58	58	65
	Don't know	11	0	0
		100	100	100

[a] After Truman's withdrawal.

only 46 percent to 43 percent. Considering that the South Dakotan won 57 percent of the delegates, this poll underscores the success of the liberals' mobilization.

The situation in 1976 was also striking. Then the liberals were Morris Udall, Jerry Brown,[6] and Frank Church; Wallace again represented the right. Although moderate Jimmy Carter was nominated, the liberals fared much better in the primaries than their numbers warranted. Primary states contributed more than 60 percent of the convention votes in 1976, and so they were far more representative of the party than in earlier years. Had the Carter consensus not piled up a huge moderate vote, the liberal advantage might well have been more evident.

The only strong candidates in 1980 were the liberal Edward Kennedy and the hero of moderates and conservatives, Jimmy Carter. The other candidates were ideologically ambiguous and lacked any strength, so I am omitting them. Kennedy ran better in the primaries than his poll showings implied, although when the "don't know" vote is excluded from the latter, the convention votes accurately reflect the Gallup totals. Perhaps Carter's status as the only incumbent in the table explains his ability to hold down Kennedy's delegate strength. It may be more remarkable that Kennedy's delegate total was as high as it was, given Carter's incumbency and the fact that Kennedy dropped out of the race two days before the balloting.

Because the differences on issues between Walter Mondale and Gary Hart in 1984 were muted, and because of the ideologically confounding role of Jesse Jackson (as discussed in Chapter 5), the race that year is not analyzed here.

Table 6.2 and the McCarthy data cited above indicate that a change in the liberals' fortunes began in 1972 and has persisted. This seems to substantiate the claim of the 1972 school that the reforms gave liberal activists a boost they had previously lacked.

The Republicans
In 1952, Robert Taft and Douglas MacArthur were the heroes of the party's right wing, and Dwight Eisenhower and several favorite sons who either endorsed him or supported him on prenomination votes at the convention represented the party's moderate-to-liberal wing. Table 6.3 shows that the right wing was unable to equal its Gallup poll strength in the primaries or at the convention. While

we lack trustworthy data from the 1940s, the success of the Wendell Willkie and Thomas Dewey campaigns suggests that 1952 was no fluke.

In 1964, Barry Goldwater was the conservative champion, but his experience was the reverse of Taft's. A Gallup-poll showing that never rose above 22 percent of Republicans was parlayed into a 38 percent share of the primary vote and a landslide victory at the convention. Even when, in June, the Gallup surveyers forced a choice between Goldwater and his chief competitor, William Scranton, Scranton won by 60 percent to 34 percent. In 1968, counting Richard Nixon as the moderate and Ronald Reagan as the conservative, with a collection of favorite sons loosely allied with the liberal Nelson Rockefeller, we can see in Table 6.3 that again the right wing was overrepresented in the primaries and at the convention. The 1976 campaign pitted the conservative Reagan against Gerald Ford, the champion of moderates and liberals (despite his conservative record and platform). Once again, the conservatives did considerably better in the primaries and at the convention than they did in the Gallup poll.

The Republican picture clearly validates the party-decline thesis, as the trend of greater conservative mobilization began in 1964 and has continued ever since. Indeed, it might be dated from the 1960 convention when Barry Goldwater exhorted conservatives to "grow up" and take over the party. But if the party-decline thesis best explains the Republican trend, and the 1972 thesis fits the Democratic data, shall we infer that Republican party leaders lost strength before the Democratic chieftains did? There is a great deal of plausibility in this argument, since the Republicans have been the minority party since the 1930s and were out of power in the 1960s when the trends toward party decline reached full impact. In that situation, party leaders may not have had as many resources for controlling the party as the Democrats did. If this is so, then the same line of reasoning might apply to the Democrats, who were not out of power until the 1972 convention. But then the liberals' gains in 1972 might have been at least equally due to the party's nonincumbent status as to the McGovern-Fraser reforms. I will not push this argument further, but it is worth stressing that any attempt to explain the advent of liberal Democratic activists by the reforms is going to have to deal with the parallel but earlier rise of conservative Republican activists.

TABLE 6.3. Showings of Republican ideological factions in Gallup surveys, primaries, and first-ballot convention votes, selected years, 1952–1976

		Gallup (%)	Primaries (%)	Convention (%)
1952:	Conservatives	46	36	42
	Moderates and Liberals	53	64	58
	Don't know	1	0	0
		100	100	100
1964:	Conservatives	17	38	68
	Moderates and Liberals	77	62	32
	Don't know	6	0	0
		100	100	100
1968:	Conservatives	9	44	14
	Moderates	52	45	52
	Liberals	34	11	34
	Don't know	5	0	0
		100	100	100
1976:	Conservatives	36	47	47
	Moderates and Liberals	57	53	53
	Don't know	7	0	0
		100	100	100

What Offices Do Nominees Hold?

There appear to be clear trends and fashions in where Presidential nominees are found—in Congress or in the statehouses. In the twentieth century until 1960, Rossiter's rule about governors was widely observed. In fact, if we look only at first-time nominees who were not incumbents, every Democratic nominee from 1912 to 1952 was a sitting governor, except for John W. Davis in 1924. While the Republicans were more eclectic in their sources of nominees, three of their first-time nonincumbent nominees from 1896 to 1952 were gubernatorial incumbents, and another, Charles Evans Hughes, had been one. The two Republican Vice-Presidents in the period who succeeded to the Presidency were former governors as well. Only two Republican nominees in this period had ever served in Congress. Indeed, from 1896 to 1956, only one incumbent member of Congress, Warren G. Harding, was nominated by either party.

This abruptly changed in 1960. Each nominee of both parties from 1960 through 1972 had been a U.S. Senator, and none had been a governor. Then, starting in 1976, the age of the governors, Carter and Reagan, returned. The first-time nonincumbent nominees from 1976 through 1984 were those two candidates and Walter Mondale.

These familiar trends can be explained to a great extent by the party-decline model. In the days before 1960, when party leaders ran conventions, among the strongest leaders were incumbent governors whose control of state patronage enabled them to secure a strong base for their candidacies (see Chapter 3). Then as parties became weaker and governors became less important figures at conventions, the pendulum began to swing toward the Senate. Senators have several advantages over governors in this new era. They are the focus of national media attention, they deal with foreign policy, and most of them have more flexible schedules than governors, who are bogged down in administrative tasks.[7] A good example of the last point is Jerry Brown's experience in 1976, when legislative commitments kept him out of the primaries until it was too late to stop Carter, despite a strong showing in the late primaries.

If senators have such advantages, how do we explain the accession of Carter and Reagan? Perhaps the key to their victories is not that they were governors but that they were *former* governors, just as Nixon and Mondale were *former* Vice-Presidents. The nominating process has become so wide open that a great deal of campaigning and organizing is necessary (see Chapter 2), and politicians have awakened to that fact:

I've learned something. You can't do your job in Congress and run for President.

—Aide to Morris Udall, 1976 campaign[8]

I never could have spent so much time campaigning like this when I was governor.

—Ronald Reagan, 1975[9]

What I considered my greatest asset in the Presidential campaign—a record of experience and performance in the Senate—actually turned into my greatest liability.

—Robert Dole, 1980 [10]

Senator Baker says he is beginning to wonder if one has to be unemployed to run for President.

—News report, 1980 [11]

To come in [to the 1984 campaign] at this point means that I would be a day late and a dollar short.

—Morris Udall, February 1983 [12]

In fact, there is empirical evidence that the more a politician is on the road, the better he or she does in the Presidential race. We can see this in observing the attendance records of members of Congress who sought the Presidency in recent years, for the year *prior* to the convention year, when organizing was most critical.[13] In 1971, George McGovern had a lower attendance rate than Shirley Chisholm, Hubert Humphrey, Henry Jackson, or Edmund Muskie—52 percent—and he was nominated. In 1975, Morris Udall had a lower rate than Birch Bayh, Frank Church, or Henry Jackson—47 percent—and came in second, far ahead of his congressional colleagues. In 1979, John Anderson had a lower rate than Howard Baker, Philip Crane, or Robert Dole—28 percent—and ran better than all of them. In 1983, however, the pattern was broken: Ernest Hollings had a higher rate of absenteeism than Alan Cranston, John Glenn, or Gary Hart; indeed, Hart's absenteeism was lowest.

Because of the absenteeism factor, congressional *leaders* are poor bets to be nominated, and commentators often lament that fact. The error is in assuming that the exclusion of congressional leaders from a serious shot at the nomination is something new. As Stephen Hess notes, "The record of legislative leaders who have caught White House fever is one of total disaster—Champ Clark, Oscar Underwood, John Nance Garner, Alben Barkley, Robert Kerr, Arthur Vandenberg, Robert Taft, William Knowland, Lyndon Johnson (1960), Wilbur Mills, Henry Jackson."[14] Rowland

Evans and Robert Novak treat Johnson's two tries for convention glory as jokes.[15] In 1980 and 1984 two new examples were added: Howard Baker and Alan Cranston. While journalist David Broder argued that Republican organization leaders would have preferred to nominate Baker, the evidence is otherwise. A poll of Republican national and state committee members in January 1980 gave Baker only 6 percent.[16]

By and large, this bias against legislative leaders, as detrimental as it may be to the election of a President who works well with Congress, may be an inevitable corollary of the divided system of American government, with separate channels of recruitment for different branches. There is a kind of symmetry here: Henry Jackson lost the Presidential primaries, and Jimmy Carter lost many battles with Congress. This is nothing new in American politics, and it cannot be blamed on new rules.

On the general question of the recent trend from senators to governors, I would argue that there is nothing inevitable about it. Indeed, I have found no member of the 1972 school who argues that the reforms caused that particular change. After all, from 1960 to 1972 there were several prominent governors—Reagan, Nelson Rockefeller, George Romney, William Scranton, and George Wallace—who were serious Presidential possibilities, and Carter and Reagan had to defeat prominent members of Congress in order to win their nominations. What does seem likely is that people with a lot of time to spare—such as members of Congress without leadership responsibilities and former governors—will have an edge over their rivals.

This subject would not be complete without a discussion of the Vice-Presidency. Until 1960, the last time an incumbent Vice-President was nominated for the White House was in 1836. Every Vice-President since 1940 has in some sense aspired to the Presidency: Garner, Wallace, and Barkley tried but failed; Nixon, Humphrey, and Mondale followed their Vice-Presidencies with Presidential nominations; Truman, Johnson, and Ford succeeded to the White House; Agnew's and Rockefeller's widely discussed ambitions were thwarted; and Bush is highly likely to seek the office in the future.

The party-decline school can explain why in 1960 there began a series of Vice-Presidents with seriously regarded White House ambitions. At a time when party leaders can no longer pull a dark horse out of their hats, the publicity given to the Vice-President is a major asset in the campaign. They may be "Spiro who?" or "Fritz who?" when nominated, but not for long. Moreover, Vice-Presidents have been claiming foreign-policy experience through their travels and other responsibilities, and they have perhaps the most flexible schedules in Washington.

Indeed, the premium on name recognition has propelled to prominence a group hitherto even more obscure than Vice-Presidents— defeated Vice-Presidential nominees. Nearly every one of them since 1960—Lodge, Muskie, Shriver, Dole, and Mondale—has mounted a Presidential campaign four years later, with Mondale winning his party's nomination and Lodge and Muskie achieving some limited success in that endeavor. In September 1979 the Gallup survey discovered that Dole was the fourth best-known of the 1980 Republican hopefuls.[17] Earlier in this century, only Franklin D. Roosevelt and Earl Warren emerged from a Vice-Presidential defeat to play a significant role in Presidential politics.

It now seems clear that the Vice-Presidency is being used to groom future Presidential hopefuls. In prior years, the nomination was used as a reward for elderly wealthy contributors; now, says Jay Hurwitz, "we see an increasing tendency in both parties for vice presidential nominees to be younger than their presidential running-mates."[18] Every Democratic ticket from 1896 to 1936, except the Cox-Roosevelt pairing in 1920, combined a younger Presidential nominee with an older Vice-Presidential nominee. The years 1940 to 1960 were a transitional era in which half the tickets had a younger Vice-Presidential hopeful, and every ticket since 1964 has had a younger Vice-Presidential aspirant. The Republicans made a cleaner break. Every ticket from 1904 to 1948 except Harding-Coolidge in 1920 had an older Vice-Presidential nominee, and every ticket since 1952 except Nixon-Lodge was the reverse. These developments clearly did not need new rules to occur.

Nominating the Vice-President

If Vice-Presidents and Vice-Presidential nominees have become a prime source of future Presidential aspirants, then the selection of

Vice-Presidential nominees becomes an especially important one. Because of the autocratic way in which the selection of a running-mate has been made, the nature of this decision has changed little over the years. Only five times since 1896—at the Democratic conventions of 1896, 1912, 1944, and 1956 and the Republican convention of 1924—has the Vice-Presidential selection required more than one ballot, and in each of those exceptions there was no clear directive from the Presidential nominee.

As a result, except for the change in ages cited above, there has been little change in the types of Vice-Presidential nominees chosen over the years. Since 1928, for example, Congress has been the most frequent source of such nominees for both parties. Except for Henry Wallace, every nonincumbent Democratic nominee since then has been a sitting member of Congress, and five of the eleven nonincumbent Republican nominees have also been from Capitol Hill. If the Ford and Rockefeller selections are included, the ratio is six out of thirteen, and the Shriver designation would be an exception to the Democratic rule.

Another twentieth-century development has been that renominated Presidents keep their running-mates on the ticket, a departure from nineteenth-century custom.[19] The only exceptions to the modern rule were unusual cases—Franklin D. Roosevelt's third and fourth terms and unelected Gerald Ford and his unelected Vice-President, Nelson Rockefeller. Moreover, had he lived, John Kennedy clearly intended to retain Lyndon Johnson in 1964.[20] Perhaps the tendency cited above for parties to consider Vice-Presidents serious Presidential possibilities has encouraged them to remain on good terms with their Presidents in order to be Vice-President during the President's second term.

Considerations of balance still play a major role in filling out the ticket. Eleven of the fifteen Democratic tickets since 1928 have included one nominee from a Southern or border state and one nominee from outside those regions. Republicans in the same period have tended to favor a Northeast–Far West combination; if Richard Nixon is consistently regarded as a Westerner, seven out of fifteen tickets involved such a pattern, and only two tickets lacked someone from either region. Religion has been a consideration in recent years, with five tickets since 1960 including a Protestant and a Roman Catholic. However, this is not mandatory; neither party chose a Catholic for either office in 1976 or 1980. Ideological balance is still a factor, as the Carter-Mondale and Reagan-Bush tickets demonstrate. Moreover, Presidential nominees who perceive themselves as centrists tend to choose similar running-mates, as both Nixon and Humphrey did in 1968.

The unprecedented nomination of a woman for Vice-President by a major party in 1984 merits special attention. It is far too early, as of this writing, to assess the long-term impact of Geraldine Ferraro's selection, but some foolhardy speculation may be in order. The same Democratic feminists who so effectively lobbied for Ferraro in 1984 will undoubtedly be heard from in the future, and concern about the "gender gap" will probably put similar pressure on Republican Presidential nominees. If women running-mates therefore become more the rule than the exception, there will be a number of conceivable consequences. For one, each party will be under some compulsion to promote its women candidates for high elective offices such as governors and senators lest a future Vice-Presidential nominee be subjected to the criticism Ferraro received that she lacked enough experience for the job. It will be in the interest of the national parties to assist their best women candidates in overcoming the gap in fund-raising and other resources that have hitherto hurt women candidates.

If women candidates are likely to benefit from the effects of the Ferraro nomination, young male aspirants to the Presidency may find one route to the White House blocked off. Numerous bright young male senators, for example, have hoped to follow in the footsteps of Richard Nixon in 1952 and be catapulted into the national limelight by a Presidential nominee. The most recent successful such aspirant was Walter Mondale. In the future, any male Presidential aspirant may have to go for broke and run for the White House directly rather than wait for a Vice-Presidential nomination that is exceedingly unlikely. This could lead to a proliferation of Presidential candidacies by men roughly in the position of Gary Hart in 1984—attractive but underfunded and unseasoned.

What else is sought in a running-mate? Although legislative leaders, as noted earlier in this chapter, are never nominated for President, they have provided a frequent source of Vice-Presidential nominees—Speaker Garner; Majority Leaders Curtis, Barkley, and Johnson; Minority Leaders Robinson and McNary (and Ford, for that matter); and Majority Whip Humphrey. This provides a signal to Congress and to the party establishment that the Presidential nominee wants to build bridges. Another way to build bridges to party leaders is to select a present or former national party chairman, as three recent Republican nominees—Goldwater, Ford, and Reagan—have done. This may be the only recent trend, and it reflects the fact that outsiders are increasingly likely to be nominated as President and *need* bridges built.

What is *not* usually sought in a running-mate is someone who already has widespread popular appeal and can bring large numbers of voters to the fold. Presidential nominees do not want to owe their running-mates that much or to have Vice-Presidents with independent power bases. William Carleton was quoted in the first chapter as predicting that the Vice-Presidential nominee would be the runner-up in the Presidential race, but that has happened only three times in American history—the Tilden-Hendricks team in 1876, the Kennedy-Johnson ticket of 1960, and the Reagan-Bush combination in 1980. (The Stevenson-Kefauver ticket was exceptional, for Stevenson did not choose Kefauver.) Other Vice-Presidential nominees have had wide followings, including Lodge in 1960 and Humphrey in 1964; still others, such as Garner in 1932, have played important roles in the Presidential nomination. But most Vice-Presidential nominees elicit from most voters the response "Who's he?"

Perhaps one aspect of the new era in Presidential nominations helps to explain why Presidential nominees do not turn to their defeated rivals when looking for running-mates. As candidates for the White House no longer vie with each other to woo party leaders, the sense that they are all part of the same party team tends to diminish. Without strong party leaders to set limits on the divisiveness of the conflict, and with ideology increasingly exacerbating intraparty tensions, nominating campaigns often become bitter.[21] There is no way to measure this empirically over time, but if it is increasingly so, it may be harder for Presidential nominees to swallow the hurt caused by the attacks of their vanquished foes and ask one of them to join the ticket, and it may be harder for the foe to agree to serve. There is evidence, for example, that in 1964 Barry Goldwater considered offering the second spot on the ticket to William Scranton but that the Scranton camp's campaign tactics offended Goldwater so much that he decided against it.[22] The possibility of a Mondale-Hart ticket in 1984 may have been precluded by similar considerations.

There is no evidence, then, of any fundamental changes in Vice-Presidential selection in the past half-century.

Conclusions

Presidential nominees are indeed different types from what they were thirty years ago. Perhaps most important, they are more likely to be ideologues; they are also much more diverse in their personal backgrounds in terms of religion, home state, and other factors; and they are highly unlikely to be sitting governors any more. All these changes can be explained by the weakening of the bonds of party leadership, and nearly all of them antedated the McGovern-Fraser reforms.

Have we gained or lost by these changes? Whether it is advantageous for us to nominate, and sometimes elect, ideologues for the Presidency is a complex matter far beyond the scope of this book. Perhaps ideological candidacies are divisive and inspire social tensions among Americans, and ideological Presidencies run the risk of rigidity and extremism. On the other hand, perhaps ideological candidacies give the American people a real choice and renew their commitment to the party system, and ideological Presidencies are the only way to shake up archaic political practices in Washington and get the nation on a new course.[23] I am not going to get into this hoary debate here, but note simply that the questions are more than academic now that three ideologues have been nominated, and one of them elected to the White House.

Far less controversial are the fallen barriers based on the "availability" criteria that reflected the prejudices of an earlier day and were irrelevant to the requirements of the Oval Office. If Roman Catholics, small-state residents, the divorced, Southerners, and others are no longer automatically barred from nomination, we have taken a step forward, and those who pine for the days of boss-dominated conventions should consider ways to block this particular aspect of bygone days from recurring. A bit less clear is the latter-day stricture against sitting governors. As with Catholicism and small-state status, gubernatorial incumbency seems to be an irrelevant criterion for exclusion; indeed, it has been argued that governors get excellent training for the Presidency with their administrative responsibilities and the necessity of working with their legislatures. On the other hand, as Carter and Reagan showed, gubernatorial experience is in itself no bar. One simply must wait until one's term is over to step up to the Presidency.

Once nominated, the man (and I use the word literally, to remind us of one irrational barrier still up) is as firmly in control of the convention as he ever was. This has not changed, and it helps to explain why the only significant remaining act of the convention, the Vice-Presidential nomination, is conducted much as it has been for decades.

SEVEN

Effects of the Process

As important as the nomination of the President is, any consideration of significant changes in the process must look beyond the convention itself to how the nominating system might affect the greater political system. Here questions of causality become much more complex, for in earlier chapters I was able to treat the nominating process somewhat artificially as a finite system that was affected by what economists call exogenous factors but that could be studied largely apart from its environment. Now the task is to look directly at that environment and how it might be affected by the subsystem that has been my main concern here. In effect, my emphasis in this chapter will be on functional rather than causal explanation. Explaining change in the wider political system may seem herculean, but if we keep in mind the finite task of this study, the task is not as daunting. We can ask of the wider world what we asked of various aspects of the nominating process: Did change occur, and if so, when? In particular, did the change precede or follow the McGovern-Fraser and subsequent reforms?

Although philosophers can argue that everything in the wider political system, as well as in other American social systems, is affected by change in the Presidential nominating process, I shall look at two of the most proximate—political parties and the Presidency. Conventions are creatures of the parties, institutions established by the major parties for a century and a half to conduct necessary business, and political scientists should not be surprised to see the parties' creations turning around and transforming their parents. Conventions also produce Presidents, and if Chapter 6 was correct in pinpointing changes in the characteristics of the nominees produced by conventions, we should not be surprised to see changes in the behavior of the occupants of the Oval Office.

Weakening the Parties

Nelson Polsby has noted the decline of partisanship and voter turnout in recent years and has speculated that the nominating reforms may have contributed to these trends. He points to two hypothetical causes: the encouragement of "factionalist struggles" that make the average citizen feel ignored and the "steady replacement of face-to-face, primary and geographically proximate interest groups with distant, symbolic and noninteractive mediation mechanisms."[1] If true, this is a serious indictment indeed, for if reform is destroying partisanship, then the parties are weaker as electoral institutions, and if turnout is declining, then the reformers' goal of increasing participation has been undermined. There is no question that the trends Polsby discusses have occurred, but when did they begin?

In Table 7.1 we can see exactly when the decline of partisanship and turnout in Presidential elections began. The proportion of the electorate which considers itself independent of party affiliation rose from 1968 to 1972 by six percentage points, which would seem to confirm Polsby's suspicions. However, it also rose 7 percent from 1964 to 1968, which seems to absolve the reforms of responsibility. These are the only real changes in this index. As for turnout, it is true that the largest decline in the table occurred from 1968 to 1972, but it was clearly part of a long-term trend, and surely the passage of the Twenty-sixth Amendment giving eighteen-to-twenty-year-olds the vote was a major factor in that development.

Unifying the Parties

Christopher Arterton, William Cavala, and James Ceaser have all suggested that the new rules and the process surrounding them may make it more difficult for supporters of losing candidates to unite behind the winner in the fall—Arterton because they might

TABLE 7.1. Percentage of voters identifying as independents, and percentage of eligible voters voting in Presidential elections, 1960–1980

Year	Independents	Turnout
1960	23	62.8
1964	22	61.9
1968	29	60.9
1972	35	55.2
1976	36	53.5
1980	35	52.6

SOURCES: For *independents*, University of Michigan Survey Research Center and Center for Political Studies, reprinted in William H. Flanigan and Nancy H. Zingale, *Political Behavior of the American Electorate*, 5th ed. (Boston: Allyn & Bacon, 1983), p. 46.

For *turnout*, Elections Research Center, reprinted in the 1982–1983 *Statistical Abstract*, p. 489.

see the rules as stacked against them, Cavala because party elites will become disgruntled at being excluded, and Ceaser because a decentralized process has relatively little legitimacy.[2] Without singling out the rules as a cause, Denis Sullivan and his colleagues suggest that candidate-centered movements produce delegates with so much psychological commitment to their candidate that they find it harder to support the winner than did the less emotionally involved delegates of an earlier age.[3] Nelson Polsby argues that the Republicans, being more ideologically cohesive than the Democrats, will suffer less from this effect than their opponents will.[4] This is an important issue, for if the rules indeed resulted in more divided parties, they have done a disservice to the parties in a critical area: the party's ability to contest elections effectively.

Measuring this phenomenon over time is difficult, and I am beginning with a fairly simple measurement of party unity: how many partisans voted in November for candidates other than their party's nominee. The reader may object that this measurement is affected by factors besides the degree of intraparty strife—for example, the presence of a strong third candidate in November or an unusually popular or unpopular major-party opponent—and that another index of dissatisfaction, nonvoting, is omitted. To the first objection, I can only say that I shall be looking at long-term trends, and to the second I cite the monotonic decline in turnout since 1960, which makes nonvoting a questionable indicator to use. Moreover, if the defeated candidate's supporters stay home on Election Day, this will serve to increase the share of the party's vote that goes to the opposition.

Table 7.2 shows Gallup survey results since 1952, and for the Democrats the peak years of defection were 1952, 1968, 1972, 1980, and 1984. While each has an explanation—Eisenhower's and Reagan's popularity, the Wallace and Anderson campaigns, McGovern's and Carter's unpopularity—the general upward trend did not begin in 1972. For the Republicans, the peak years were 1964, 1968, and 1980; Goldwater's unpopularity and the Wallace and Anderson efforts are relevant here. By and large, an upward trend affected the Republicans as well, and again it did not begin in 1972. Moreover, it is consistent with the ocean of evidence that suggests a less partisan electorate than earlier.[5]

Another test of the postconvention unity of parties is the extent

TABLE 7.2. Percentage of partisans voting for candidates other than one's party's nominee in November, 1952–1984

Year	Democrats	Republicans
1952	23	8
1956	15	4
1960	16	5
1964	13	20
1968	26	14
1972	33	5
1976	18	9
1980	31	14
1984	21	4

SOURCES: For 1952–1980, *Gallup Opinion Index*, no. 183 (December 1980), pp. 6–7.
For 1984, Gallup Poll press release, November 7, 1984.

TABLE 7.3. Fellow partisans' support of Presidential nominees in the general election, by whether they supported other candidates before the nominating convention, 1964–1984

Year and party	Supported nominee, or no preference	Supported other candidate	Difference	Signifi-cance, by chi-square test
1964 Rep.	77.2%	67.5%	+ 9.7%	a
1968 Dem.	69.0	72.1	− 3.1	a
1968 Rep.	91.1	82.7	+ 8.4	a
1976 Dem.	83.3	65.3	+18.0	.001
1976 Rep.	87.7	72.5	+15.2	.01
1980 Dem.	81.5	60.0	+21.5	.02
1980 Rep.	98.8	64.7	+34.1	.001
1984 Dem.	85.3	72.1	+13.2	.001

SOURCE: University of Michigan Survey Research Center and Center for Political Studies Surveys.

[a] Not significant at .05 level.

to which those supporting candidates who lost the nomination were likelier to defect in November than those who supported the winner. For example, were Democrats who supported Edward Kennedy in 1980 less likely to vote for Jimmy Carter in November than were Democrats who backed Carter before the convention? The University of Michigan surveys enable us to answer this question for each contested convention from 1964 to 1984, except for the Democrats in 1972, and they give us data for the Republicans in 1980 as well. The results are in Table 7.3, and they seem to bear out the 1972 school's expectations better than Table 7.2 did. Both in absolute terms (the third column of data in Table 7.3) and by a common test of statistical significance (the fourth column), post-1972 conventions reveal greater differences between supporters of the nominee's rivals and the rest of the party than pre-1972 conventions did.

The evidence on whether the new rules have resulted in more

divided parties is mixed, and we need more elections to ascertain whether the idiosyncrasies of the years I have examined explain the trend that appears so marked in Table 7.3.

Nationalization of Parties

Another important trend that is as difficult to quantify as it is controversial is the increasing nationalization of party politics. Everyone who discusses this subject agrees that our parties are significantly more nationalized today than they were a couple of decades ago. The national parties, particularly the Democrats, have asserted far more power over state parties' delegate selection procedures. This trend was first ratified in 1972, when the Supreme Court granted the national party the authority to override state party procedures. Judicial decisions since then have given national party rules precedence over state statutes as well.[6]

As the Court's decision in 1972 was an outgrowth of the controversy over the McGovern-Fraser reforms, it is tempting to assert that the increased nationalization of parties was a result of the 1972 reforms; Christopher Arterton, William Crotty, John Kessel, and Nelson Polsby have done so.[7] After all, the very existence of the reform commissions was an indication that the national parties were going to start playing a more assertive role in politics. Others—James Ceaser, Jeane Kirkpatrick, and Gerald Pomper— have acknowledged that although the new rules might have accelerated the process, we can trace recent nationalizing tendencies to 1956, when the Democrats instituted a loyalty oath, or to 1964, when a "compromise" over Mississippi's racial practices was reached by the convention.[8] Xandra Kayden sees longer-term forces at work on the parties, accelerated by the FECA.[9] Austin Ranney is inconsistent on this point, citing the 1956 and 1964 events (calling them "minor") but then referring to the 1972 rules as "the first increase in the power of a party's *national* organs since . . . 1824."[10]

My position is that the nationalization of our parties has been a gradual process lasting well over a century. Although recent rules changes have indisputably accelerated that nationalization in unprecedented ways, these changes cannot be appreciated without understanding the longitudinal trend. In order to argue this point, I must expand on the notion of nationalization, and for support I turn to James Madison in the thirty-ninth *Federalist* paper:

The House of Representatives will derive its powers from the people of America; and the people will be represented in the same proportion and on the same principle as they are in the legislature of a particular State. So far the government is *national*, not *federal*. The Senate, on the other hand, will derive its powers from the States as political and coequal societies; and these will be represented on the principle of equality in the Senate, as they now are in the existing Congress. So far the government is *federal*, not *national*.[11]

Here Madison's use of "national" implies more than national power only; it involves the equality of persons and the absence of intervening levels of government. A truly nationalized polity will not only concentrate power in the national government, but in order to preclude rival political institutions from competing with it, it will try to ensure political equality among the citizens. If some citizens are "more equal" than others, they can form a bloc, perhaps a powerful state government, that can threaten national supremacy. Are citizens equal, and acted on directly by the national government (as Hamilton advocated in the sixteenth *Federalist* paper), or are they to be regarded primarily as members of states, and the states regarded as equals regardless of their populations? These are important questions in considering the meaning of nationalization and the history of party conventions.

Nineteenth-Century Developments

The first major-party national conventions in 1831 replaced congressional caucuses and represented a devolution of nominating power from federal to state and local party leaders.[12] The Democrats, the "states' rights" party, leaned toward a federal model from the outset. First, each state received a number of convention votes equal to its electoral votes, regardless of how many Democrats lived there. Of course, the electoral college also tends to equalize the states by giving each a minimum of three votes. The second rule that expressed the federal orientation was that each delegation cast its votes as a delegation, without individual delegates casting ballots as was done at the Anti-Masonic and National Republican conventions in 1831. This reinforced the notion that delegates were to be regarded less as individuals than as parts of state delegations. Third, the unit rule enabled the states that adopted it to vote in a bloc and override the wishes of delegates in the minority; this rule not only subsumed individual rights under states' rights but also increased the power of states that exercised the option, as they were fatter prizes for candidates. Finally, the two-thirds rule, in conjunction with the unit rule, meant that a winning candidate usually had to amass an overwhelming majority of states, and not merely pull together a collection of individual delegates from here and there. This system may well have fostered the emphasis on sectionalism that was so important at that time by encouraging candidates to concentrate their resources in friendly states, ignoring states in which their supporters were clearly in the minority. Moreover, it was a system similar to the electoral college, which has long been considered a bulwark of states' rights, and an almost Calhounian system whereby nearly every major interest in the party had to approve the nominee. The Whig party did not adopt the unit or two-thirds rule, befitting its status as the more "nationally" oriented party,[13] but in delegate apportionment and in the casting of votes by delegation, it followed the precedent set by the Democrats.

Gradual moves toward the nationalization of both parties ensued. In 1848 the Democratic convention established the Democratic National Committee, to be composed in federal fashion of one member from each state, "to promote the Democratic cause." In 1866 the Democrats and Republicans both set up congressional campaign committees, and as early as 1880 the Republican National Committee claimed the right to decide contests for its membership.[14]

The Republicans, a party less wedded to states' rights in the last century than the Democrats were,[15] demonstrated their greater propensity for nationalization in their rules. Like the Whigs, they never adopted the two-thirds or unit rule, enabling candidates to win in nationalized fashion by amassing portions of delegates from many states to secure a bare majority of the convention total. Convention rhetoric reflected interparty differences on this score. In 1876 a Republican orator asked whether the state of Pennsylvania shall make laws for this convention; or whether this convention is supreme and shall make its own laws. We are supreme. We are original. We stand here representing the great Republican party of the United States.[16]

Four years later a Democratic delegate defended the unit rule by excoriating the Republicans as

a party which believes . . . that the states have hardly any rights left which the Federal Government is bound to respect . . . [and] that the state does not control its own delegation in a national convention. Not so in the convention of the great Democratic party. We stand, Mr. President, for the rights of the states.[17]

Despite these differences, both parties' conventions leaned heavily in the federal direction. Like the Democrats, the Republicans allocated delegation strength by electoral vote, had votes cast by state delegation, and gave states equal representation on the national committee. This reflected the generally weak role of the federal government in American life, and the strength of state and local party machines.

Twentieth-Century Developments

From a nineteenth-century federal phase, the parties gradually became more nationalized in the twentieth century. I attribute the underlying causes to the transportation and communication revolutions, greater centralization of government power in Washington and in the Presidency, and the ensuing nationalization of American politics in general.[18] These trends were reflected in new party rules. The development of the Presidential primary may not have been fundamentally a nationalizing phenomenon, but it may have encouraged party members to think of themselves as individuals with a role to play rather than as members of a state organization. Far more important to my argument was the creation of bonus votes, appropriately in the more nationally oriented Republican party in 1916. The "System of 1896" had sectionalized American politics to an almost unprecedented extent, and many Republicans protested the inequity of giving the South, which had cast 7 percent of the Republican Presidential vote in 1908, nearly one-fourth of the votes at national conventions. Bonus votes, which were given to states that had supported the party's ticket in the last general election, began to provide for state representation on the basis of *individual partisans*, instead of on the state's role in the political system at large. This different kind of representation would have been recognized as more national by Madison. The Democrats followed suit, but only after the two-thirds rule was abolished. This deprived the South of one of its major weapons, although the institution of bonus votes gave the region a substitute.[19]

The effect of bonus votes must not be exaggerated, however. For one thing, they were usually not a major factor; in 1956, for example, they comprised only about 18 percent of the vote at both parties' conventions.[20] Second, all states, regardless of their size, were eligible for the same number of bonus votes, so that the votes had an equalizing effect on the states that received them.

The Democrats' abolition of the two-thirds rule in 1936 followed three conventions whose nominating battles exceeded forty ballots and the near-denial of the nomination to Franklin D. Roosevelt in 1932 despite his securing nearly 60 percent of the vote on the first three ballots. Abolition of the rule marked a watershed in several ways, for it reflected the growing liberalism and nationalism of the party under Roosevelt.[21] Since then, that party has been more nationalistic than the Republican party, and unlike in earlier eras the Democrats have initiated most rules changes.

The first indication of this came in 1952, after a number of Southern state parties had refused to support the Truman-Barkley ticket in 1948. Northern liberals persuaded the 1952 convention to pass a proposal requiring that all delegates pledge to "exert every honorable means" to get the nominees for President and Vice-President on the ballot as the official Democratic candidates in the states; if not, they would not be seated at the convention.[22] After passing this "loyalty oath" resolution, however, the convention also voted to seat three noncompliant Southern delegations for the sake of party unity. The party subsequently adopted three rules for its 1956 and 1960 conventions: that each state party "undertakes to assure" that the national ticket would appear on the state ballot under the official Democratic designation (by citing the party instead of the delegates, the Democrats separated this issue from the delegate-certifying process); that no loyalty oath would be required of delegates; and that the National Committee could expel any of its members who did not support the national ticket (which officially sanctioned a practice that had occurred in the past). In 1958 the National Committee even overruled the Louisiana state organization's firing of a National Committeeman who was regarded as too liberal on civil rights.[23] By and large these rules were not revolutionary, but as Abraham Holtzman noted, they marked "a transitory step toward the nationalization of that party" and "the growing governing function of national conventions."[24] State parties were slowly losing power to the national party, and the process continued through the party's first gingerly refusal to admit all-white delegations from the Deep South in 1964 and 1968 and the use of the loyalty oath in the prior year.[25]

This brings us to the current period, when these episodic and often groping moves became major efforts to bring state parties in line with national party mandates. By my earlier criteria of nationalization too, this process has accelerated within the Democratic party: the unit rule was abolished in 1968, and the delegate apportionment formula in recent years gives equal weight to electoral votes and to the number of votes cast in recent Presidential elections for the Democratic nominee (see Chapter 5). This means that half the apportionment is on the basis of Democratic *voters*, and not simply the total population of the states. But the historical precursors should not be overlooked. The Republicans' refusal to adopt the two-thirds and unit rules, the establishment of national party committees, the adoption of bonus votes, the Democrats' abolition of the two-thirds rule, and that party's loyalty controversy in the 1950s were all steps in the direction of nationalization broadly understood. That this development had acquired momentum by the late 1960s is reflected in the fact that the Democratic convention of 1968, so tightly controlled by the party organization, voted to abolish the unit rule and set up what became the McGovern-Fraser Commission. That commission sent the nationalizing trend into orbit, but we would be making a mistake if we did not acknowledge the long-term factors at work.

Presidential Behavior

I have suggested that if in recent years we have had kinds of nominees different from those of the past, then it stands to reason that the behavior of these people once they reach the White House will also be different. This may be the most important question in this entire book, for if we find that rules changes are producing poorer performance by American Presidents, then that in itself will persuade many that the rules are a disaster. James Ceaser argues that the candidate-centered nominating process discussed in Chapter 3 produces what he calls the "Wilsonian executive":

one who is "free" of party (but who cannot thereby call on it to aid him in winning public support), one who may raise great expectations about what a president as an individual can accomplish, and one who is led to emphasize authority based on an informal relationship with the people rather than the authority of the office itself.[26]

Donald Fraser sees the primaries producing less cohesion among elected officials, and Austin Ranney states flatly that the new rules reduce nominees' dependence on party leaders and that therefore Presidents "seem even less likely than ever before to succeed in—or even attempt—drives for party unity among presidentially-led congressional parties."[27]

If I have correctly argued in Chapter 3 that candidate-oriented campaigns have long been a part of the scene, then we should expect to see quite a few recent Presidents resemble the type that Ceaser, Fraser, and Ranney see coming from the new system. And there is much evidence that this is so.[28] It should not be surprising that the citizens' movement that advanced Eisenhower produced a President well known for eschewing overt partisanship. His television coaching by Robert Montgomery, his cooperation with Democratic congressional leaders Lyndon Johnson and Sam Rayburn, and his lack of coattails in 1956 are all indicators of a President who placed himself "above partisanship" and sought a direct relationship with the people.

John Kennedy is a more difficult case to analyze. On the one hand, he had what David Broder calls an "equivocal" relationship to his party, willing to use it only when it served his interests.[29] In the words of Donald Robinson, Kennedy "did almost nothing . . . to strengthen the Democratic National Committee" and concentrated political power in the White House.[30] Kennedy's reliance on his own personal political resources is illustrated by his use of pollster Louis Harris. On the other hand, Broder argues that Kennedy was preparing for a Presidential race in 1964 that would stress interparty differences, promote a realignment, and thus strengthen the Democratic party.[31]

There is less ambiguity in the record of Lyndon Johnson, who in many ways was the least partisan of all—dominating and eviscerating the Democratic National Committee, stressing consensus over interparty differences, concentrating power still further in the White House staff, distrusting collegial political structures, using the polls as evidence of a personal relationship with the electorate.[32]

Richard Nixon, long regarded as an extremely partisan figure, followed the Johnson pattern to a remarkable degree—concentrating political power in the White House staff, running campaigns totally divorced from the party and relying on personal loyalists, duplicating Johnson's "consensus" strategy in 1972, and ignoring the Republican National Committee.[33]

In short, Broder and Robinson agree that we have not had a true "party government" President at least since Harry Truman, unless Kennedy's aspirations for his second term are taken seriously. We can even wonder whether Kennedy would have deemed it to be in his interest to be a strongly partisan President, for none of the other Presidents of the 1953–1974 period did so. It is becoming increasingly clear that we have not been the victims of coincidence in having so many apartisan Presidents, but that the decay of partisanship in general and concomitant developments have given Presidents few incentives to behave in partisan ways. The voters are less likely than before to respond to Presidential partisanship, fellow partisans in Congress can get elected and reelected without the President's coattails, and the bureaucracy is largely insulated from the appointive (and dismissive) power. Whether all this is for better or worse—and I am as troubled about it as Ceaser and Ranney are—it is an evolutionary development and cannot be blamed on rules changes.

Another bit of evidence of this secular trend can be found in an incisive comparison of the chief executive selection processes in Great Britain and the United States by Hugh Heclo. Heclo termed the American nominating process "entrepreneurial" and suggested that it produces a President who will "pay greater attention to public preferences in justifying his actions" and is more individualistic than British prime ministers, who are "nominated" by a party caucus in the House of Commons.[34] What is especially pertinent here is that Heclo's penetrating analysis was published in 1973, and it made no distinction between George McGovern and earlier Presidential nominees. This would seem to demonstrate that this American pattern long antedated the McGovern-Fraser reforms.

Finally, a bona fide member of the 1972 school, Edward Banfield, corroborates my argument. Describing the "new" nominating system, Banfield suggests that the President will be estranged from his party's leaders in Congress and that he will rely on public relations merchandising. Yet he goes on to say that "the Republican party was gravely damaged by Eisenhower's neglect," that Adlai Stevenson brought "amateurs" with a weak sense of partisanship into the Democratic party, and that John Kennedy's campaign "demonstrated how little the party professionals had come to matter."[35] Surely Eisenhower and Kennedy experienced friction with their respective party leaders in Congress, and both relied on public relations gimmickry and, in Kennedy's case especially, the polls. Banfield's description of the dire effects of the new nominating system apply equally well to the earlier Presidents he cites. And even Nelson Polsby, who bases his claims for the effects of the reforms on one case, that of Jimmy Carter, acknowledges that Carter's neglect of "mediation processes" was foreshadowed in the Nixon Presidency.[36]

Conclusions

Have the new rules nationalized the parties, grievously divided them, and produced "loner" Presidents who are ill-equipped to work with fellow partisans? Only the first trend can be linked squarely to the post-1968 reforms, and even there it was part of a long historical development. The evidence on party disunity is mixed, and suffers especially from limited data. As for the caliber of our chief executives, the Presidential traits that have been linked to the reforms were evident in the White House for twenty years before the reforms were enacted. Surely Ronald Reagan's success with Congress in 1981 shows that the new system need not preclude Presidential effectiveness at achieving legislative goals.

Except for nationalization of parties, which was part and parcel of the new rules, studying these developments runs into the serious methodological difficulties noted at the beginning of this chapter. Have other factors, such as the increasing ideologization of the American electorate,[37] been responsible for the greater apparent disunity of our parties? Has the loosening of the bonds between President and party been accelerated by the new rules, and how can we measure this? It is not surprising that this chapter has methodologically been the most problematic of the book.

EIGHT

Some Implications for Future Reformers

Wº hat effect have recent nominating rules changes had on the political process? Throughout this volume, I have listed numerous changes that were not caused primarily by these reforms, and a much smaller number of what I would argue are less significant changes that were clearly occasioned by the new rules. I have also presented a number of ambiguous cases, but even if a hard-liner of the 1972 school were to argue that *all* such ambiguous cases were caused by the rules, the total list would still be much smaller than that implied by the inflated rhetoric of the 1972 school.

Specifically, the new rules seem clearly to have caused, directly or indirectly, a lengthening of the race; the proliferation of primaries; changes in the demography, the experience, and the degree of unity of Democratic delegations; and an acceleration of the nationalization of the Democratic party. On the other hand, longer-term forces were at work in causing a decline in uncommitted delegates, favorite sons, and the number of nominating ballots; the rise of candidate organizations; incumbents' greater difficulty at winning nomination; variations in the attendance of Democratic members of Congress and Republican governors as delegates; greater factional persistence; the decline of "availability" considerations; more ideological Republican nominees; fewer incumbent gubernatorial nominees; the decline of partisanship and electoral partic-

141

ipation; and less party-oriented Presidential behavior. There has seemingly been little or no change in the number of candidates running; the front-runner's ability to win nomination; the relationship of prenominating ballots to the Presidential race; the attendance of Democratic governors and Republican senators; the inability of congressional leaders to win nomination; and Vice-Presidential selection. Finally, ambiguous cases include the degree of power of governors and leaders of national party organizations at conventions; the attendance of Republican House members; the incidence of ideological Democratic nominees; and postconvention party unity.

My conclusion, then, is that even if the McGovern-Fraser Commission and its successors had never held a meeting, we would have ended up with roughly the system we now have. I say "roughly" because I have never argued that the rules had no impact whatsoever. I do claim, however, that the Reagan nomination was foreshadowed by the Goldwater nomination, and the Carter nomination of 1976 in some important respects by the Kennedy nomination of 1960, the Eisenhower nomination of 1952, and the Willkie nomination of 1940. In all these instances, party leaders were unable to stop the nomination of political "outsiders."

In this study I have been criticizing the work of numerous able and respected colleagues, and the reader may well wonder, if my analysis is correct, how so many intelligent people could have been laboring in the wrong vineyard. Why has so much ink been wasted on debating the rules if the rules played at best a secondary role in these changes? Austin Ranney has suggested that while the rules were not everything, they *are* about the only aspect of the system that is easily manipulable.[1] This would make sense if one believed that by manipulating the rules the process could be substantially changed. But as I shall argue, that is far from clear.

Denis Sullivan and his colleagues argue that Democratic conservatives have singled out the rules for opprobrium in order to discredit their liberal foes, those responsible for the changes, and to rally the factions sympathetic to themselves.[2] Of course, Sullivan et al. might also have suggested the "functional" significance of emphasizing the reforms for those who, like themselves, advocate the reforms. For example, Democratic liberals might exaggerate the impact of the reforms in order to take credit for trends of which they approve, and to rally *their* allies.

All these reasons may provide psychic justification for giving the reforms more responsibility for change than they deserve. I would add another, *political* reason. Conservatives of the sort identified with the American Enterprise Institute like to fancy themselves spiritual heirs of Edmund Burke. Suspicious of rationalistic attempts to reshape society and its institutions, they are quick, like Edward Banfield, to cite the organic nature of society and the dangers of stirring up unforeseen consequences when we meddle with it.[3] When reformers such as the McGovern wing of the Democratic party, with whom these conservatives have many disagreements on political and cultural matters irrelevant to my concerns here, attempt just such a transformation, conservatives look for the deleterious unforeseen consequences, and as they seek, they shall find. In particular, they find a nominating process that by the mid-1970s had come under attack from a wide swath of the ideological spectrum, and from there it took little time—indeed, too little time—for the conservatives to ascertain that the reforms *caused* this controversial new system. It would have been far more difficult for them to admit that this organic society they cite has been organically evolving to the present nominating system. Far more comfortable to blame it on woolly-headed reformers and their tinkering.

Liberals have an equal and opposite blind spot. The faith of modern liberalism is that we *can* tinker with institutions, and although unforeseen consequences are always a threat, we can end up with a better system than the one with which we started. Just as conservatives saw recent party reforms as evidence that rationalistic reformism is doomed to failure, liberals saw those same reforms as evidence that rationalistic reformism has positive consequences. In this respect, both sides have a stake in the importance of reform—conservatives to show that reform has damaged the national interest, liberals to show that it has bettered our world. The underlying consensus is that the rules were efficacious at *something*. On the contrary, I have argued, the rules were not primarily responsible for change in the process.

There are some important consequences of our answers to these questions, and they involve whether the system can be transformed by human will back to the halcyon days before the McGovern-Fraser reforms. Members of the 1972 school argue that what the rules gave with one hand they can take away with the

other. In an attack on the new nominating process, David Broder
has written:

The good news is that there is nothing sacred about this kind of presidential selection system. It has not been ordained by God, nor inscribed
in the Consitution, nor legislated by the Congress, nor mandated by the
courts. It is a political artifact, of recent design, which can be changed
by relative ease by two of the most accessible, persuadable bodies of
decision-makers in the land: the Democratic and Republican National
Committees.[4]

Acknowledging that many of the causes of party decline are not
manipulable, James Ceaser suggests at least reducing the number
of primaries and amending the FECA.[5] On the other side of the
debate, Sullivan and his colleagues deny that going back to the old
system would be politically feasible or desirable, but they do not
deny that it may be possible.[6] As for myself, I agree most with
David Adamany, who gently criticized "a wishfulness that Humpty
Dumpty could be put back together again by changing statutes,
which in the scheme of things is a much easier task than reversing
basic changes in society."[7]

But the very desire to reverse these changes by statute has led to
a crop of proposals, many of which incorporate Ceaser's program
noted above. These are at best an indirect way to restore state and
local party leaders to their place of eminence at conventions, and I
prefer to consider more direct restorations. In 1973 the Coalition
for a Democratic Majority, a conservative Democratic lobby, called
for "state parties to choose a larger percentage of a state's convention delegates."[8] The party followed suit for the 1980 convention
by expanding each delegation's size by 10 percent in order to include party and public officials, as noted in Chapter 4. Since then,
others have upped the ante. Broder calls for 25 percent of the delegation to be party leaders, and Laurence Radway wants half to be.[9]
Everett Ladd wants a nationwide primary to select two-thirds of
each party's delegates and the remaining delegates to be chosen
from party and public officials serving ex officio.[10] The Democrats
increased the proportion of officials by adopting the report of their
Commission on Presidential Nomination, commonly known as the
Hunt Commission after its head, Governor James Hunt of North
Carolina. The commission, whose report was adopted in the spring

of 1982, proposed to add to the aforementioned 10 percent several hundred unpledged delegates who would be party and public officials, raising those officials' percentage of the total delegates to about 22 percent.[11]

I question whether such measures will achieve their goal, to add an element of cautious deliberation to the proceedings. (They did not in 1984.) I suspect that such deliberation over the merits of possible Presidents was never characteristic of conventions even when leaders were in control, at least if we recall several important points about those conventions. One is the difficulty of deliberating in large assemblies of any kind. As Madison reminds us in the fifty-fifth and fifty-eighth *Federalist* papers, large assemblies experience "the confusion and intemperance of a multitude . . . the ascendancy of passion over reason."[12] Numerous observers of turn-of-the-century conventions agreed, Woodrow Wilson declaring that "there is no debate in nominating conventions, no discussion of the merits of the respective candidates, at which the country can sit as audience and assess the wisdom of the final choice."[13] Of course, the hoopla, the confusion, the invasion of journalists, the difficulty of securing privacy, and fatigue make the national convention an improbable forum for genuine deliberation.

On the other hand, it is conceivable that leaders used to meet in smoke-filled rooms to carry on serious deliberation about the relative merits of candidates. More likely, they met to discuss patronage and campaign plans and looked for a candidate whose electability was more important than his potential for statesmanship. In the words of Lord Bryce, "What a party wants is not a good President but a good candidate."[14] Bryce and other observers of the period agreed that the criterion of electability led to a preference for "safe" candidates who had never said, nor would be likely to say, anything that might offend any bloc of voters—hardly the kind of criterion likely to produce a high standard of Presidential leadership. Moreover, as noted in Chapter 6, electability meant "availability," discrimination against many candidates because of their religion, home state, and other attributes unlikely to be correlated with statesmanship.

If most observers are correct in stating that party leaders wanted electability above all else, then the new system may involve a departure from that norm by producing nominees who are highly popular with party activists but unpopular with the electorate en masse. Pointing to the nominations of Stevenson and Humphrey, Kenneth Bode and Carol Casey note that party leaders also pick losers,[15] but this is an unfair argument. The more appropriate question is whether, say, Kefauver or McCarthy would have run *better* than Stevenson or Humphrey, not who would have won. (Could any Democrat have defeated Eisenhower?) Table 8.1 shows several recent cases in which the organization tended to favor one candidate while the primaries produced another. The Gallup survey compared how each candidate ran against the other party's nominee close to the convention, and the results appear in Table 8.1.[16] In every case except 1972 (when there was no difference), the choice of the *primary* voters was more popular than the choice of party leaders, as far as the general electorate was concerned.

What are we to infer from Table 8.1? One possibility is that the party leaders believed, despite the polls, that their favorite would run a better race in November. Certainly the tendency for the polls to rise and fall with the success or failure of candidates in the primaries[17] might have created a "halo" effect for Kefauver, McCarthy, McGovern, and Carter. A shrewd party leader might have regarded Stevenson, Humphrey, and Mondale as having more "staying power." Yet I cannot help thinking that a rational leader would have used the polls as the best "hard" evidence of candidates' relative standings with the electorate, especially in 1952 and 1968 when there was a sizable difference between how the candidates ran.

Another possible explanation of the data in Table 8.1 is that we are observing conditions as the decline of the bosses was well under way. Perhaps in an earlier age, when they controlled the process completely, leaders were more serious about electability; today they indulge their sentimental favorites knowing that their preferences will not be determinative anyway. This is even less plausible than the previous argument. The 1952 and 1968 conventions *were* controlled by party leaders, and there was much effort by leaders in 1972 and 1976 to stop the front-runner. Moreover, the leaders' choices in those years were entirely logical ones for organization stalwarts to make.

I am drawn to a third possibility, that electability was not the most important criterion. Like the fabled post-office Republicans of the Old South, party leaders are known to be willing to sacrifice victory in favor of controlling the organization: better to lose with

TABLE 8.1. Selected Gallup survey "trial heats," comparing Democratic organization favorites and primary winners, 1952–1984

Year	Organization favorite		Primary winner	
1952	Eisenhower	59%	Eisenhower	55%
	Stevenson	31	Kefauver	35
	(Difference	28)	(Difference	20)
1968	Nixon	45	Nixon	42
	Humphrey	29	McCarthy	37
	Wallace	18	Wallace	16
	(N − H	16)	(N − M	5)
1972	Nixon	52	Nixon	53
	Humphrey	32	McGovern[a]	34
	(Difference	20)	(Difference	19)
1976	Humphrey	48	Carter	49
	Ford	46	Ford	43
	(Difference	2)	(Difference	6)
1984	Reagan	53	Reagan	51
	Mondale	42	Hart[a]	44
	(Difference	11)	(Difference	7)

SOURCES: *The Gallup Poll*, vol. 2 (New York: Random House, 1972), pp. 1069–1070, and the following editions of the *Gallup Opinion Index*: no. 39 (September 1968), pp. 10–11; no. 84 (June 1972), pp. 6, 8; no. 129 (April 1976), pp. 8–9; and no. 225 (June 1984), pp. 18–19.

[a] Won most primaries; rival won most votes.

Humphrey than to win with McCarthy and have the President or his supporters depose you as state chairman. Moreover, even if survival is not a problem, a party leader wants a President who will cooperate on matters of patronage. Stevenson, Humphrey, and Mondale, one might suppose, would be more cooperative than Kefauver, McCarthy, McGovern, Carter, or Hart, all of whom expressed their attitude toward the party establishment when seeking the nomination by ignoring or attacking various leaders. My conclusion is that winning is no more an exclusive criterion for party leaders than it is for other activists, a point supported empirically for the 1972 Democratic convention by Sullivan and his colleagues.[18] Party leaders are looking for winners who will coop-

erate with them whenever a U.S. attorneyship or a federal judge-
ship opens up. This is the goal of their "deliberations."

For the moment, however, let us assume that the leaders would
add an element of deliberative wisdom to the convention. This implies several things. First, it implies that the leaders would be a
relatively homogeneous lot who could unite on a candidate, or at
least promote a set of candidates different from the ones produced
by the primaries. Otherwise, why add them to the delegates? Indeed, a CBS News survey of the delegates to the 1984 Democratic
national convention found that when the uncommitted and unpledged were removed, there was virtually no difference on candidate preference between those delegates who were party or elected
officials and those who were not.[19] Second—and this is the crucial point—this argument assumes that if such unity was possible
the leaders would have the courage to overturn the winner of the
most primaries. If they were successful, their candidate would be
the candidate of the "bosses" rather than the candidate of the
"people," and as William Howard Taft learned in 1912 and Hubert
Humphrey learned in 1968, this is a damaging image to bring into
a campaign. Moreover, a party leader who participated in such a
coup would be in danger of being overthrown in the future by
those whose desires were ignored at the convention. How many
leaders would stick their necks out that far? Besides the Taft and
Humphrey experiences, we have the situation in recent years in
New York, once a state with strong parties. Since 1968, Democratic
candidates for statewide office have first vied for the endorsement of
the state committee, and then everyone who either received a certain proportion of the committee vote or secured enough petitions
could contest the nomination in a primary. Organization-backed
candidates lost six out of the nine primaries for governor or senator from 1968 to 1982 (two of the three winners were incumbents). In 1974, all of the four primaries (for state attorney general
and controller as well as for governor and senator) resulted in defeats for the organization. In 1980 the state committee made no
endorsement for the Senate, perhaps not wishing to give anyone
the kiss of death. I suspect that even if the party leaders whom
Broder, Radway, Ladd, and the Hunt Commission want to send
to the convention could unite on a candidate different from the
winner of the primaries, their endorsement would have the same
impact as the New York State Democratic Committee's.[20]

This example demonstrates the folly of trying to overturn an evolutionary social phenomenon by tinkering with rules. The cause of the new system is not that too few party leaders are attending conventions or that those who do attend control too few votes; that is the *effect* of other, more fundamental changes. It is a symptom. Increasing the number of party officials will not restore Richard Daley, Leonard Hall, John Bailey, or Marcus Alonzo Hanna. It will send to the convention "leaders" who lack resources, underlings, and allies, knights to battle in an age of gunpowder.

While I have concentrated on measures to increase the participation of party and public officials, the other major recommendations of the Hunt Commission can be similarly questioned. For example, the relaxation of proportional representation requirements at most took the system back to 1972, when the new process was well under way. The removal of binding pledges for many delegates similarly took the system back to 1976; even in 1980, when the rule was a major issue for the Democrats, it was unlikely that "freeing" the delegates would have changed the outcome of the balloting. Most delegates in recent years have been fervent advocates of their preferred candidates, as Senator Edward Kennedy demonstrated when he dropped out of the race and saw nearly all his delegates vote for him anyway.[21] Finally, the proposal to shorten the process to a fifteen-week affair may be a blessing to a supersaturated public, but it is unlikely to affect the balance of forces. After all, in 1964 Barry Goldwater was nominated in a process that took only twelve weeks to overthrow his party's establishment. We have no more eloquent testimony to the inefficacy of the Hunt Commission's attempt to turn back the clock than that its proposals were endorsed by George McGovern himself.[22] And the convention that ensued was a typical latter-day affair, with the winner already selected in the primaries, and two insurgent candidates winning more than 42 percent of the delegates between them.

If the reforms were not responsible for most of the changes in the nominating process, and if therefore repealing or changing the reforms will not negate these developments, what is the significance of the reforms? In Chapter 1, I tentatively suggested that the reforms may have been a filling of the vacuum left by the decline of party, in order to routinize and legitimize the new process. Here I would like to develop that idea, with the understanding that it is not the sort of theory that is easily verifiable with empirical evidence.

In an earlier age, authority and a kind of moral accountability were easily located at national conventions in the party leaders who controlled them. It may be an overstatement to say that these leaders were vested with legitimacy, because antibossism has long been an important strain in the American political culture, but at least they were tolerated as controllers of the nominating process, and only sporadic attempts to increase the number of primaries challenged their authority. When that authority began to wane, for reasons that had little to do with the Presidential nominating process, newer and less easily identifiable groups began to displace them. Candidate cadres, adherents of incumbents, constituency groups, and ideological factions became more important, but there were no routinized patterns of access to convention power, nor were these disparate groups vested with formal legitimacy.

The reforms have provided such routinization and legitimacy. New primaries and caucuses, each with carefully defined rules guaranteeing access for any well-mobilized group, rules for dividing delegations fairly among the claimants, and new agencies of appeal and review all provided routinized access to the convention. They also conferred legitimacy on whoever made best use of these access routes. McGovern-Fraser Commission member Austin Ranney has often commented that the proliferation of primaries was an *unintended* consequence of that commission's rules,[23] but my argument suggests why primaries proliferated: they fit Americans' populistic notions of legitimacy so well that they were the most logical way to legitimize the new system. By 1980 even the caucuses were treated as quasi-primaries, with returns reported in the media as though they were primaries. By 1976 the Iowa caucuses began to equal the New Hampshire primary in psychological impact.

Legitimacy was also conferred in other ways, most notably by provisions that delegates declare their Presidential preferences early (thereby legitimizing candidate cadres) and the affirmative-action rules (which legitimized the mobilization of the affected groups). Not only did affirmative action legitimize the increased presence at the convention of these groups, but it also helped legitimize the new convention as a whole. While representation takes many forms,[24] one that is notably salient in politics is the physical representation of key groups in numbers roughly equivalent to their proportion of the total population. Since most Americans regard representation as a major element of legitimacy, this increased actual representation can only serve to increase the legitimacy of the convention and hence the nominating process.

Finally, it is striking that the American political system's chief institution for conferring legitimacy, the federal judiciary, has ratified the rules whenever possible. It has upheld both parties' delegate apportionment formulas,[25] approved with relatively peripheral modifications the Federal Election Campaign Act,[26] and permitted national party rules to override state law.[27] Moreover, the Supreme Court indirectly ratified longer campaigns by requiring television stations to grant advertising time to candidates regardless of when the station deems the campaign has begun.[28] While I do not mean to imply that the courts have been in cahoots with party elites, their stamp of approval strengthens the legitimacy of the rules and therefore the process.

Indeed, by 1980 even William F. Buckley Jr. cited the "rule" that primaries have been the determining factor in the nominating process as "a stabilizing factor in American politics," and as a self-styled conservative he approved of this function.[29] I am not arguing that legitimization was a conscious and overriding goal of the reformers, only that sooner or later something was needed to perform this function.

So the reforms are the new system's answer to those who asked about the new power centers, "Who gave *them* the right to choose the nominee?" They also lay the ground rules for competition among those power centers. But it would be a serious mistake to infer, as so many have, that these rules *created* the game—they simply codified the way in which it would be played.

In order to provide more credibility for my explanation for the new rules, I shall discuss for a moment the shortcomings of three other possible explanations. The first is the one given most often by the champions of the rules, that the rules were caused (and justified) by the abuses of the nominating process by leaders of the Democratic party in 1968. There is some historical precedent for the notion that controversial nominations lead to rules changes. The Republican convention of 1912, for example, with the pivotal role played by Southern delegations, gave impetus to the "bonus vote" system, and the lengthy Democratic conventions in 1912, 1920, and 1924 eventually helped to persuade the party to drop the two-thirds rule. The heavy-handed tactics of the Johnson administration forces at the 1968 Democratic convention, including non-recognition of dissidents, strategically timed adjournments, and the dictation of the platform, as well as the nomination of a candidate who was untested in the primaries, surely contributed to the reform impulse. Moreover, such practices as steep fees for delegates, obscure delegate selection rules, and delegates being chosen the year before the convention gave more ammunition to the reformers. But if the Humphrey nomination caused the McGovern-Fraser Commission, then why did the Stevenson nomination of 1952 not cause a similar groundswell of reform? After all, the supporters of Estes Kefauver had even more reason than the supporters of Eugene McCarthy to cry foul: Kefauver had won twelve out of sixteen primaries in 1952, while McCarthy only won six out of fourteen in 1968. The answer, it seems to me, is that the waning of party organizations had not reached a critical point by 1952.

Another alleged cause of the reforms, cited most often by their critics, is that the reforms were essentially a power play by the activists to take over the nominating process. This theory relies heavily on the fashionable notion that a "new class" of highly educated professionals with liberal views has become a new elite in American society. Everett Ladd writes:

In fact, it has been upper-middle-class groups, not the broad mass of Americans, who have confronted the party organizations, who have held them to be unresponsive to their policy perspectives, who have attacked the legitimacy of "bosses," who have urged "democratization." And it is these highly educated, well-informed, relatively prosperous groups who have primarily benefited from party "reform," for they tend to participate in more open nomination processes at a rate that far exceeds that of "rank-and-file-citizens." [30]

The problem with this theory as the main explanation for the new rules is that the advent of the "new class" must be an evolutionary process. Why was 1968 the watershed year? Again, judging from the involvement of such people in Democratic politics in the 1950s,[31] we might well wonder why this power play did not occur many years sooner than it did.

A third theory bears some similarity to mine. Theodore Lowi has suggested that the reforms are a consequence of the increased power of the Presidency in the past couple of decades: "As the presidency became more powerful there was a concomitant demand to democratize it. At a minimum this required opening up the processes of selection."[32] Again, there is some surface plausibility here, for the increases in Presidential power in the past, notably under Jackson and the two Roosevelts, were accompanied by "democratizing" reforms in the nominating process. National conventions were born toward the close of Jackson's first term, Presidential primaries began during Theodore Roosevelt's, and the Democrats' abolition of the two-thirds rule and adoption of bonus votes occurred during the administration of Franklin D. Roosevelt. However, again we must ask why the recent reforms occurred precisely when they did. Moreover, it is difficult to find evidence of what Lowi describes as a "demand" for democratization *because* of increased Presidential power.

What is ultimately unsatisfying about all three theories is the simple fact that the process has been evolving in this direction for many years, as I have demonstrated at some length. While the reformers can perhaps be excused for not recognizing this evolution in the heat of the nominating battle of 1968 and the old leadership's last gasp, a glance backward at the Goldwater nomination in 1964, the Kennedy campaign in 1960, the Eisenhower and Kefauver movements in 1952, and the Willkie drive in 1940 might have given them instructive precedents for the McGovern campaign four years later. While the neo-conservative critics are correct in noting the leadership role played by activists in the new process, that increased role seems to have come about far more through evolution than through a determined power play. Finally, Lowi may be correct that the new system helps to legitimize an often "imperial" Presidency, but I have shown that many of these trends began well before 1960, the beginning of Lowi's "Second Republic."

Any valid explanation of the reforms will have to take into account that they followed many of the most significant changes in the nominating process. Reformers and their critics often miss this crucial fact and give misleading explanations of the origin of the reforms, for those reforms were unnecessary to achieve their alleged purpose (either the elimination of "boss rule" or the increased power of the "new class"). Lowi is closer to a valid explanation, although his emphasis on post-1968 developments is similarly misleading, and the linkage between Presidential power and the nominating process is one that is not evident in the long debate over the rules changes. The rules should be seen primarily as a legitimization of prior changes, and thus indirectly legitimize the President while directly legitimizing the process that produces him.

I have not attempted in this analysis to pass judgment on the new age of Presidential nominations, for there is a voluminous literature that does this and I have cited much of it in these chapters. Many of the points made on both sides of the debate provide useful insights into the strengths and weaknesses of the system that has evolved, but as I argued earlier in this chapter, the shortcomings may be less amenable to piecemeal reform than critics assume. The reversal or alteration of the trends that I have been discussing requires changing the capabilities of our political parties, which in turn requires fundamental alterations in many major societal developments. That is the subject of a crusade, or at least another book.

Appendix: Sources of Data

Several kinds of data have not been given source citations because they were so frequently used. They are as follows:

I. Convention roll-call votes
  A. Through 1972
    Richard C. Bain and Judith H. Parris, *Convention Decisions
    and Voting Records*, 2d ed. (Washington, D.C.: The Brook-
    ings Institution, 1973).
  B. 1974 Democratic
    Sheila Hixson, ed., *The Official Proceedings of the 1974
    Conference on Democratic Party Organization and Policy*
    (Washington, D.C.: Democratic National Committee, 1974),
    pp. 180–181, 184–185.
  C. 1976
    Guide to 1976 Elections (Washington, D.C.: Congressional
    Quarterly, Inc., 1977), pp. 10–11.
  D. 1978 Democratic
    Data graciously provided the author by the Office of the
    Secretary of the Democratic National Committee, Washing-
    ton, D.C.
  E. 1980
    Congressional Quarterly Weekly Report, July 19, 1980,
    p. 2067, and August 16, 1980, p. 2436.
  F. 1984
    Congressional Quarterly Weekly Report, July 21, 1984,
    pp. 1799–1800, and August 25, 1984, p. 2128.

Occasionally the official proceedings of the convention in question were consulted.

II. Primary election returns
   A. 1912–1964
      James W. Davis, *Presidential Primaries* (New York: Thomas Y. Crowell Co., 1967), pp. 278–305.
   B. 1968
      Congressional Quarterly Almanac (Washington, D.C.: Congressional Quarterly, Inc., 1968), pp. 971–973.
   C. 1972
      Richard M. Scammon and Alice V. McGillivray, eds., *America Votes 12* (Washington, D.C.: Congressional Quarterly, Inc., 1977), p. 21.
   D. 1976
      Guide to 1976 Elections (Washington, D.C.: Congressional Quarterly, Inc., 1977), pp. 26–30.
   E. 1980
      Congressional Quarterly Weekly Report, July 5, 1980, pp. 1870–1871.
   F. 1984
      Congressional Quarterly Weekly Report, various editions.

Notes

CHAPTER 1: CAUSES AND EFFECTS

1. Most of the works cited here discuss the McGovern-Fraser reforms, but a good starting point is the commission's report, *Mandate for Reform* (Washington, D.C.: Democratic National Committee, 1970). See also William Crotty, *Party Reform* (New York: Longman, 1983).
2. On Republican rules changes, see William J. Crotty, *Political Reform and the American Experiment* (New York: Thomas Y. Crowell Co., 1977), and the following editions of *Congressional Quarterly Weekly Report*: April 29, 1972, p. 943; August 21, 1976, p. 2256; July 9, 1977, pp. 1427–1428; June 3, 1978, p. 1394; April 28, 1979, p. 777; and June 30, 1979, p. 1301.
3. On the Mikulski rules and their effects, see James W. Ceaser, *Presidential Selection* (Princeton: Princeton University Press, 1979), pp. 284–287; and Paul T. David and James W. Ceaser, *Proportional Representation in Presidential Nominating Politics* (Charlottesville: University Press of Virginia, 1980).
4. The literature on the FECA is large and growing. A useful introduction to the issues involved is Michael Malbin, ed., *Parties, Interest Groups, and Campaign Finance Laws* (Washington, D.C.: American Enterprise Institute, 1980). See also Elizabeth Drew, *Politics and Money* (New York: Macmillan, 1983).
5. Austin Ranney, "The Democratic Party's Delegate Selection Reforms, 1968–76," in Allan P. Sindler, ed., *America in the Seventies* (Boston: Little, Brown & Co., 1977), p. 163.
6. Ibid., p. 204. See also Austin Ranney, "The Political Parties: Reform and Decline," in Anthony King, ed., *The New American Political*

System (Washington, D.C.: American Enterprise Institute, 1978), pp. 236–241, esp. p. 238.

7. "Primaries '80: Once Again the System Worked, Sort Of," *New York Times*, June 8, 1980, sec. 4, p. E5.

8. Jeane Jordan Kirkpatrick, *Dismantling the Parties* (Washington, D.C.: American Enterprise Institute, 1978), pp. 2, 6. See also Jeane J. Kirkpatrick, *The New Presidential Elite* (New York: Russell Sage Foundation and the Twentieth Century Fund, 1976), pp. 45–49, 354, 365.

9. Malbin, ed., *Parties, Interest Groups*, p. 325.

10. Edward C. Banfield, "Party 'Reform' in Retrospect," in Robert A. Goldwin, ed., *Political Parties in the Eighties* (Washington, D.C., and Gambier, Ohio: American Enterprise Institute and Kenyon College, 1980), p. 23; William Cavala, "Changing the Rules Changes the Game," *American Political Science Review* 68 (March 1974): 27–42; Ceaser, *Presidential Selection*, pp. 236, 240–241, 288; idem, "Political Change and Party Reform," in Goldwin, ed., *Parties in the Eighties*, pp. 110, 114; idem, *Reforming the Reforms* (Cambridge, Mass.: Ballinger Publishing Co., 1982); Judith A. Center, "1972 Democratic Convention Reforms and Party Democracy," *Political Science Quarterly* 89 (June 1974): 325–349; David and Ceaser, *Proportional Representation*, pp. 67–69; James W. Davis, *Presidential Primaries* (Westport, Conn.: Greenwood Press, 1980), p. 74; idem, *National Conventions in an Age of Party Reform* (Westport, Conn.: Greenwood Press, 1983), p. 35; Nelson W. Polsby, *Consequences of Party Reform* (New York: Oxford University Press, 1983); Byron E. Shafer, *Quiet Revolution* (New York: Russell Sage Foundation, 1983); Stephen J. Wayne, *The Road to the White House* (New York: St. Martin's Press, 1980), pp. 90–97, 116–117; David S. Broder, "Primary Pitfalls," *Washington Post*, June 8, 1980, p. B7; and Penn Kemble and Josh Muravchik, "The New Politics and the Democrats," *Commentary*, December 1972, pp. 78–84. Polsby notes reservations about this school in *Consequences*, pp. 4–5, 132, 151–152, and 181, but the rest of his book is clearly in this camp.

11. Kemble and Muravchik, "New Politics," p. 78.

12. William J. Crotty, *Decision for the Democrats* (Baltimore: Johns Hopkins University Press, 1978), p. 254.

13. Ibid., pp. 255–262.

14. Crotty, *Political Reform*, pp. 272–273.

15. F. Christopher Arterton, "Recent Rules Changes Within the Na-

tional Democratic Party" (Paper presented to the annual meeting of the Social Science History Association, Columbus, Ohio, November 3–5, 1978), pp. 18–28; and Robert T. Nakamura and Denis G. Sullivan, "Party Democracy and Democratic Control," in Walter Dean Burnham and Martha Wagner Weinberg, eds., *American Politics and Public Policy* (Cambridge, Mass.: MIT Press, 1978), pp. 26–40. See also William Crotty, *Party Reform* (New York: Longman, 1983).

16. A general but brief treatment of these trends is William J. Crotty and Gary C. Jacobson, *American Parties in Decline* (Boston: Little, Brown & Co., 1980). Works concentrating on changes in electoral behavior include Walter Dean Burnham, *Critical Elections and the Mainsprings of American Politics* (New York: W. W. Norton & Co., 1970); Gerald Pomper, *Voters' Choice* (New York: Dodd, Mead & Co., 1975); and Norman H. Nie, Sidney Verba, and John R. Petrocik, *The Changing American Voter* (Cambridge, Mass.: Harvard University Press, 1976). For a contrary view, see James L. Sundquist, "Whither the American Party System?" *Political Science Quarterly* 88 (December 1973): 559–581.

17. The original statement of this argument is Walter Dean Burnham, "The Changing Shape of the American Political Universe," *American Political Science Review* 59 (March 1965): 7–28.

18. Data from Warren E. Miller, Arthur H. Miller, and Edward J. Schneider, *American National Election Studies Data Sourcebook, 1952–1978* (Cambridge, Mass.: Harvard University Press, 1980), pp. 81, 385, 387; and my calculations from the 1980 and 1982 American national election studies.

19. *Congressional Quarterly* data reported in John F. Bibby, Thomas E. Mann, and Norman J. Ornstein, *Vital Statistics on Congress, 1980* (Washington, D.C.: American Enterprise Institute, 1980), pp. 103–104, and subsequent editions of the *Congressional Quarterly Almanac*.

20. Data from Gene Wyckoff, *The Image Candidates* (New York: Macmillan, 1968), pp. 13–14. For speculation about the effects of television on politics, see David L. Paletz and Robert M. Entman, *Media Power Politics* (New York: The Free Press, 1981); and Austin Ranney, *Channels of Power* (New York: Basic Books, 1983).

21. Martin P. Wattenberg, *The Decline of American Political Parties, 1952–1980* (Cambridge, Mass.: Harvard University Press, 1984), pp. 92–98.

22. See Daniel Bell, *The Coming of Post-Industrial Society* (New York:

Basic Books, 1973); Samuel P. Huntington, "The United States," in Michel Crozier et al., *The Crisis of Democracy* (New York: New York University Press, 1975), pp. 59–118; and Everett Carll Ladd Jr. with Charles D. Hadley, *Transformations of the American Party System* (New York: W. W. Norton & Co., 1975).

23. See the San Francisco Bay Area Kapitalistate Group, "Political Parties and Capitalist Development," *Kapitalistate* 6 (1977): 7–38, and the essays in Claus Offe, *Contradictions of the Welfare State*, ed. John Keane (London: Hutchinson & Co., 1984).

24. Paul T. David, Malcolm Moos, and Ralph M. Goldman, *Presidential Nominating Politics in 1952* (Baltimore: Johns Hopkins University Press, 1954), 1:170, 237.

25. William G. Carleton, "The Revolution in the Presidential Nominating Convention," *Political Science Quarterly* 72 (June 1957): 237; emphasis in the original. See also idem, "How Free Are the Nominating Conventions?" *Virginia Quarterly Review* 40 (Spring 1964): 205–223.

26. Arthur T. Hadley, *The Invisible Primary* (Englewood Cliffs, N.J.: Prentice-Hall, 1976), p. 279. See also Nakamura and Sullivan, "Party Democracy," p. 36.

27. Hadley, *Invisible Primary*, pp. 7, 278, 283.

28. Theodore H. White, *The Making of the President 1960* (New York: Atheneum Publishers, 1961), p. 189.

29. For Adamany's position, see Malbin, ed., *Parties, Interest Groups*, pp. 314–316. See also John H. Aldrich, *Before the Convention* (Chicago: University of Chicago Press, 1980), pp. 8–10; Kenneth A. Bode and Carol F. Casey, "Party Reform: Revisionism Revised," in Goldwin, ed., *Parties in the Eighties*, p. 19; Donald M. Fraser, "Democratizing the Democratic Party," in ibid., pp. 121, 126–127; Xandra Kayden, "The Nationalizing of the Party System," in Malbin, ed., *Parties, Interest Groups*, esp. p. 257; Everett Carll Ladd Jr. with Charles D. Hadley, *Transformations of the American Party System*, 2d ed. (New York: W. W. Norton & Co., 1978), pp. 56–58; Robert Shogan, "The Gap: Why Presidents and Parties Fail," *Public Opinion* 5 (August–September 1982): 18; and Richard A. Watson, *The Presidential Contest* (New York: John Wiley & Sons, 1980), pp. 96–97.

30. Austin Ranney, "Changing the Rules of the Nominating Game," in James David Barber, ed., *Choosing the President* (Englewood Cliffs, N.J.: Prentice-Hall, 1974), pp. 74, 82; and idem, *Curing the Mis-*

chiefs of Faction (Berkeley: University of California Press, 1975), pp. 206–210.

31. William R. Keech and Donald R. Matthews, *The Party's Choice* (Washington, D.C.: The Brookings Institution, 1976), p. 4; see also Matthews, "Presidential Nominations," in Barber, *Choosing the President*, pp. 35–70.

32. Gerald M. Pomper, "The Decline of the Party in American Elections," *Political Science Quarterly* 92 (Spring 1977): 24.

33. James R. Beniger, "Winning the Presidential Nomination," *Public Opinion Quarterly* 40 (Spring 1976): 22–38.

34. William H. Lucy, "Polls, Primaries, and Presidential Nominations," *Journal of Politics* 35 (November 1973): 830–848, esp. 844–845.

35. Steven J. Brams, *The Presidential Election Game* (New Haven: Yale University Press, 1978); Eugene B. McGregor Jr., "Rationality and Uncertainty at National Nominating Conventions," *Journal of Politics* 35 (May 1973): 459–478; Philip D. Straffin Jr., "The Bandwagon Curve," *American Journal of Political Science* 31 (November 1977): 695–709; and James P. Zais and John H. Kessel, "A Theory of Presidential Nominations, With a 1968 Illustration," in Donald R. Matthews, ed., *Perspectives on Presidential Selection* (Washington, D.C.: The Brookings Institution, 1973), pp. 120–142. The seminal work in this area is William A. Gamson, "Coalition Formation at Presidential Nominating Conventions," *American Journal of Sociology* 67 (September 1962): 157–171.

36. Judith H. Parris, *The Convention Problem* (Washington, D.C.: The Brookings Institution, 1972), pp. 81–108.

37. Nelson W. Polsby and Aaron Wildavsky, *Presidential Elections*, 5th ed. (New York: Charles Scribner's Sons, 1980), pp. 138–143.

38. See James I. Lengle and Byron Shafer, "Primary Rules, Political Power, and Social Change," *American Political Science Review* 70 (March 1976): 25–40; Gerald M. Pomper, "New Rules and New Games in Presidential Nominations," *Journal of Politics* 41 (August 1979): 784–805; David and Ceaser, *Proportional Representation*, pp. 34–60; and Thomas H. Hammond, "Another Look at the Role of 'The Rules' in the 1972 Democratic Presidential Primaries," *Western Political Quarterly* 33 (March 1980): 50–72.

39. Kirkpatrick, *New Presidential Elite*, p. 16.

40. Ibid., p. 278. The reference is to Herbert McClosky, Paul J. Hoffman, and Rosemary O'Hara, "Issue Conflict and Consensus Among Party

Leaders and Followers," *American Political Science Review* 54 (June 1960): 405–427. For a similar error, see Everett Carll Ladd Jr., *Where Have All the Voters Gone?* (New York: W. W. Norton & Co., 1978), pp. 62–63.

41. Kirkpatrick, *New Presidential Elite*, p. 350.
42. Ibid., p. 351.
43. Polsby, *Consequences*, pp. 77, 86, 102–130.
44. Arterton, "Recent Rules Changes," p. 19.
45. Center, "1972 Reforms," p. 341; and Kemble and Muravchik, "New Politics," p. 83.
46. Kirkpatrick, *New Presidential Elite*, p. 64.
47. The figure for 1968 was computed from data in *Mandate for Reform*, p. 30; for 1972, Kirkpatrick, *New Presidential Elite*, p. 64.
48. Crotty, *Decision for the Democrats*, p. 256.
49. For definitions of "key votes" and "contested conventions," see below.
50. Stephen Hess, *The Presidential Campaign*, rev. ed. (Washington, D.C.: The Brookings Institution, 1978), p. 103.
51. Ranney, "Delegate Selection Reforms," p. 202.
52. See the University of Michigan Center for Political Studies data presented in Wayne, *Road to the White House*, p. 57.
53. On party "systems," see William Nisbet Chambers and Walter Dean Burnham, eds., *The American Party Systems* (New York: Oxford University Press, 1967).
54. This is also the operational definition used by Anne N. Costain, "An Analysis of Voting in American National Nominating Conventions, 1940–1976," *American Politics Quarterly* 6 (January 1978); 95–120.

CHAPTER 2: NOMINATING PATTERNS
1. This discussion owes much to Nelson W. Polsby, "Decision-Making at the National Conventions," *Western Political Quarterly* 13 (September 1960): 609–619.
2. Rick Stearns, quoted in Ernest R. May and Janet Fraser, eds., *Campaign '72: The Managers Speak* (Cambridge, Mass.: Harvard University Press, 1973), pp. 106–107.
3. Penn Kemble, quoted in Paul T. David and James W. Ceaser, *Proportional Representation in Presidential Nominating Politics* (Charlottesville: University Press of Virginia, 1980), p. 111.

4. Nelson W. Polsby, *Consequences of Party Reform* (New York: Oxford University Press, 1983), p. 71.
5. Denis G. Sullivan, Jeffrey L. Pressman, and F. Christopher Arterton, *Explorations in Convention Decision Making* (San Francisco: W. H. Freeman & Co., 1976), pp. 19–20.
6. See the commission's report, *Call to Order* . . . , published by the Democratic National Committee, p. 56.
7. Max Frankel, "Ho Hum, Another Last Hurrah," *New York Times Magazine*, July 11, 1976, p. 10.
8. Quoted in Adam Clymer, "Gauging the Delegate Count as the Nominations Approach," *New York Times*, May 17, 1980, p. 10. This development makes ludicrous Tom Wicker's lament that if the Carter forces won their rules fight with the Kennedy supporters in 1980, "a delegate would become not a real representative of those who elected him, acting on their behalf and accepting the responsibility for his or her actions, but an automatic vote cast in a predetermined manner"— as if delegates had been anything but that for decades. See Wicker, "What Is a Delegate?" *New York Times*, July 11, 1980, p. A25.
9. Polsby, *Consequences*, p. 77.
10. Gilligan is quoted in David and Ceaser, *Proportional Representation*, p. 10. See also William R. Keech and Donald R. Matthews, *The Party's Choice* (Washington, D.C.: The Brookings Institution, 1976), p. 234; Jeane Kirkpatrick, *The New Presidential Elite* (New York: Russell Sage Foundation and the Twentieth Century Fund, 1976), p. 365; Judith H. Parris, *The Convention Problem* (Washington, D.C.: The Brookings Institution, 1972), pp. 84–85; and Nelson W. Polsby and Aaron Wildavsky, *Presidential Elections*, 5th ed. (New York: Charles Scribner's Sons, 1980), pp. 230–231.
11. Later in this chapter I shall test the hypothesis that more candidates are *receiving votes* than ever before.
12. David and Ceaser, *Proportional Representation*, p. 111.
13. They include Keech and Matthews, *Party's Choice*, p. 87; Jeane Jordan Kirkpatrick, *Dismantling the Parties* (Washington, D.C.: American Enterprise Institute, 1978), p. 23; Polsby and Wildavsky, *Presidential Elections*, p. 150; Gerald M. Pomper et al., *The Election of 1976* (New York: David McKay Co., 1977), pp. 3–4; and Austin Ranney, "The Democratic Party's Delegate Selection Reforms, 1968–76," in Allan P. Sindler, ed., *America in the Seventies* (Boston: Little, Brown & Co., 1977), p. 195.
14. The 1980 Republican nomination, which by my definition was un-

contested and hence does not appear in Table 2.4, drew five candidates who received at least 10 percent of the vote in one primary.

15. See Herbert B. Asher, *Presidential Elections and American Politics*, rev. ed. (Homewood, Ill.: Dorsey Press, 1980), p. 285; John Kessel, *Presidential Campaign Politics* (Homewood, Ill.: Dorsey Press, 1980), pp. 251–253; Polsby, *Consequences*, pp. 59–62; Polsby and Wildavsky, *Presidential Elections*, pp. 81, 84; and the remarks of Jessica Tuchman of Morris Udall's 1976 staff in Jonathan Moore and Janet Fraser, eds., *Campaign for President* (Cambridge, Mass.: Ballinger Publishing Co., 1977), p. 152.

16. Kenneth A. Bode and Carol F. Casey, "Party Reform: Revisionism Revised," in Robert A. Goldwin, ed., *Political Parties in the Eighties* (Washington, D.C., and Gambier, Ohio: American Enterprise Institute and Kenyon College, 1980), p. 18.

17. Polsby and Wildavsky, *Presidential Elections*, p. 115.

18. Ibid., pp. 80–81. See also Donald M. Fraser, "Democratizing the Democratic Party," in Goldwin, *Parties in the Eighties*, p. 125.

19. F. Christopher Arterton, "Recent Rules Changes Within the National Democratic Party" (Paper presented to the annual meeting of the Social Science History Association, Columbus, Ohio, November 3–5, 1978), p. 22.

20. Richard C. Bain, *Convention Decisions and Voting Records* (Washington, D.C.: The Brookings Institution, 1960).

21. While significance tests may seem inappropriate when studying a universe, they have been used to measure the strength of a relationship. See Robert F. Winch and Donald T. Campbell, "Proof? No. Evidence? Yes. The Significance of Tests of Significance," *American Sociologist* 4 (May 1969): 140–143.

CHAPTER 3: WHO CONTROLS THE NOMINATIONS?

1. See Paul T. David, Ralph M. Goldman, and Richard C. Bain, *The Politics of National Party Conventions* (Washington, D.C.: The Brookings Institution, 1960), pp. 96–99; and Gerald Pomper, *Nominating the President* (New York: W. W. Norton & Co., 1966), pp. 131–133.

2. Senator Robert Taft, quoted in David et al., *Politics of Conventions*, p. 556.

3. Senator John McClennon, quoted in Arthur M. Schlesinger Jr., *Rob-*

ert Kennedy and His Times (New York: Ballantine Books, 1978), p. 142.

4. Donald M. Fraser, "Democratizing the Democratic Party," in Robert A. Goldwin, ed., *Political Parties in the Eighties* (Washington, D.C., and Gambier, Ohio: American Enterprise Institute and Kenyon College, 1980), p. 126.

5. Nelson W. Polsby and Aaron Wildavsky, *Presidential Elections*, 5th ed. (New York: Charles Scribner's Sons, 1980), p. 108.

6. The data are summarized in William R. Keech and Donald R. Matthews, *The Party's Choice* (Washington, D.C.: The Brookings Institution, 1976), p. 238.

7. See *U.S. News & World Report*, November 17, 1975, p. 24; February 16, 1976, p. 17; and February 18, 1980, p. 42; and *Newsweek*, March 26, 1984, p. 22.

8. See *U.S. News & World Report*, January 28, 1980, p. 59. On the Republican governors in 1980, see David S. Broder, "Grand Old Patsies," *Washington Post*, May 25, 1980, p. B7.

9. On incumbents' relationships with nominating conventions in general, see my "The Gavels of August: Presidents and National Party Conventions," in Robert Harmel, ed., *Presidents and Their Parties* (New York: Praeger Publishers, 1984), pp. 96–121.

10. Some historians even suggest that, in 1884, Chester Arthur did not seriously seek the nomination because he was dying of a kidney ailment. See "President Arthur Kept Illness a Secret," *New York Times*, September 18, 1972, pp. 1, 22.

11. Johnson denied that he intended to stay in the race. See his *The Vantage Point* (New York: Popular Library, 1971), chap. 18. If he intended to withdraw, why did he allow his supporters to wage the fight in New Hampshire? See also Doris Kearns, *Lyndon Johnson and the American Dream* (New York: Signet Books, 1976), chap. 12. A good analogy is with the Truman situation in 1952; Truman also claimed to have decided to withdraw long before his defeat in New Hampshire. See *Memoirs by Harry S. Truman: Volume II, Years of Trial and Hope* (New York: Signet Books, 1965), pp. 551–556.

12. On Carter's use of his incumbency, see David S. Broder, "Jimmy Carter's 'Good News' Strategy," *Washington Post*, April 6, 1980, p. E7; Timothy B. Clark, "As Long As Carter's Up He'll Get You a Grant," *New York Times*, April 21, 1980, p. A19; Elizabeth Drew, "1980: The President," *The New Yorker*, April 14, 1980, pp. 121–169; Terence Smith, "The Selling of the President," *New*

York Times Magazine, February 24, 1980, pp. 24ff.; and Steven R. Weisman, "White House Visits: New Campaign Tool," *New York Times*, March 13, 1980, p. A21.

13. Jonathan Moore and Janet Fraser, eds., *Campaign for President* (Cambridge, Mass.: Ballinger Publishing Co., 1977), p. 33. In the same volume, see also the comments of Reagan aides Lyn Nofziger and David Keene on pp. 43 and 151 respectively.

14. Ibid., p. 39.

15. Edward C. Banfield, "Party 'Reform' in Retrospect," in Goldwin, ed., *Parties in the Eighties*, p. 25.

16. E. E. Schattschneider, *Party Government* (New York: Rinehart & Co., 1942), p. 206.

17. "Primaries," editorial in *New York Times*, April 9, 1920, p. 12; *Public Papers of the Presidents of the United States: Harry S. Truman, 1952–1953* (Washington, D.C.: Government Printing Office, 1966), p. 132; and Stevenson is quoted in David et al., *Politics of Conventions*, p. 296.

18. James W. Davis, *Presidential Primaries* (New York: Thomas Y. Crowell Co., 1967), pp. 108, 249.

19. F. Christopher Arterton, "Recent Rules Changes Within the National Democratic Party" (Paper presented to the annual meeting of the Social Science History Association, Columbus, Ohio, November 3–5, 1978), pp. 20–21; James W. Ceaser, *Presidential Selection* (Princeton: Princeton University Press, 1979), p. 294; Judith A. Center, "1972 Democratic Convention Reforms and Party Democracy," *Political Science Quarterly* 89 (June 1974): 345; William J. Crotty, *Decision for the Democrats* (Baltimore: Johns Hopkins University Press, 1978), pp. 255–257; Paul T. David and James W. Ceaser, *Proportional Representation in Presidential Nominating Politics* (Charlottesville: University Press of Virginia, 1980), pp. 68–69; Jeane Kirkpatrick, *The New Presidential Elite* (New York: Russell Sage Foundation and the Twentieth Century Fund, 1976), pp. 46, 48; idem, *Dismantling the Parties* (Washington, D.C.: American Enterprise Institute, 1978), pp. 6–8; Everett Carll Ladd Jr., *Where Have All the Voters Gone?* (New York: W. W. Norton & Co., 1978), pp. 56–58; Robert T. Nakamura and Denis G. Sullivan, "Party Democracy and Democratic Control," in Walter Dean Burnham and Martha Wagner Weinberg, eds., *American Politics and Public Policy* (Cambridge, Mass.: MIT Press, 1978), p. 34; Judith H. Parris, *The Convention Problem* (Washington, D.C.: The Brookings Institution,

1972), p. 84; Nelson W. Polsby, "The News Media as an Alternative to Party in the Presidential Selection Process," in Goldwin, ed., *Parties in the Eighties*, pp. 54–55; idem, *Consequences of Party Reform* (New York: Oxford University Press, 1983), pp. 67–68, 72–73; Gerald M. Pomper et al., *The Election of 1976* (New York: David McKay Co., 1977), p. 4; Austin Ranney, *Curing the Mischiefs of Faction* (Berkeley: University of California Press, 1975), p. 154; and idem, "The Democratic Party's Delegate Selection Reforms, 1968–76," in Allan P. Sindler, ed., *America in the Seventies* (Boston: Little, Brown & Co., 1977), p. 195.

20. Ladd, *Where Have All the Voters Gone?* p. 57.
21. Donald Bruce Johnson, *The Republican Party and Wendell Willkie* (Urbana: University of Illinois Press, 1960), pp. 64, 66–67.
22. David S. Broder, *The Party's Over* (New York: Harper & Row, 1971), pp. 6, 22.
23. Theodore H. White, *The Making of the President 1960* (New York: Atheneum Publishers, 1962), p. 52.
24. Broder, *The Party's Over*, pp. 23–24, 25.
25. Robert D. Novak, *The Agony of the G.O.P. 1964* (New York: Macmillan, 1965), pp. 345–346.
26. Aaron Wildavsky, "The Goldwater Phenomenon," *Review of Politics* 27 (July 1965): 386–413.
27. On the growing independence of the electorate, see note 16 for Chapter 1; on the rise of amateur activists, see James Q. Wilson, *The Amateur Democrat* (Chicago: University of Chicago Press, 1962); and on new campaign technology, see Larry Sabato, *The Rise of Political Consultants* (New York: Basic Books, 1981).

CHAPTER 4: WHO ARE THE DELEGATES?

1. For data through 1944, see Marguerite J. Fisher and Betty Whitehead, "Women and National Party Organization," *American Political Science Review* 38 (October 1944): 896.
2. Numerous scholars, activists, and journalists have estimated the demographic background of delegates over the years. For the sake of space, I am citing only one source per datum, with the assurance that practically all estimates cluster close together. The data on women delegates in 1952 and 1956 come from Paul T. David, Ralph M. Goldman, and Richard C. Bain, *The Politics of National Party*

Conventions (Washington, D.C.: The Brookings Institution, 1960), pp. 327–328, and for the Democrats in 1956, my own calculation from the official roster of delegates; for the Democrats in 1960 and 1964, official party data cited in Stephen J. Wayne, *The Road to the White House* (New York: St. Martin's Press, 1980), p. 93; for the Republicans in 1960 and 1964, my own calculations from the official rosters of delegates; for 1968 through 1980, CBS News data reported in Warren J. Mitofsky and Martin Plissner, "The Making of the Delegates, 1968–1980," *Public Opinion* 3 (October–November 1980): 43; and for 1984, *New York Times*, August 24, 1984, p. A10. Mass data were from the University of Michigan Survey Research Center and Center for Political Studies (hereafter SRC/CPS) surveys and, for 1984, the CBS News survey of September 30 to October 4.

3. Sources of data on black delegates were the following: for 1952, David et al., *Politics*, p. 329; for 1964, *Mandate for Reform* (Washington, D.C.: Democratic National Committee, 1970), p. 26, and *The Presidential Nominating Conventions 1968* (Washington, D.C.: Congressional Quarterly Service, 1968), p. 222; for 1968 through 1980, Mitofsky and Plissner, "Making of the Delegates," p. 43; and for 1984, *New York Times*, August 24, 1984, p. A10. Mass data were from the University of Michigan SRC/CPS surveys and, for 1984, the CBS News survey of September 30 to October 4.

4. Data from Part A of Table 4.3 are from the following sources: for 1968 and for the Democrats in 1972, CBS News data graciously provided by Kathleen A. Frankovic; for the Republicans in 1972, Joseph H. Boyett, "Background Characteristics of Delegates to the 1972 Conventions," *Western Political Quarterly* 27 (September 1974): 472; for 1976, *Washington Post*, August 15, 1976, p. A6; and for 1980, *Washington Post*, August 11, 1980, p. A9. Data from Part B of Table 4.3 are from the following: for 1948, David et al., *Politics*, p. 561; and for 1968 through 1980, Mitofsky and Plissner, "Making of the Delegates," p. 43; and for 1984, *New York Times*, August 24, 1984, p. A10. Mass data were from the University of Michigan SRC/CPS surveys and, for 1984, the CBS News survey of September 30 to October 4.

5. See the previous footnote for the source of those data, and also *Congressional Quarterly Weekly Report*, August 12, 1972, p. 1998. A much higher estimate of Republican youth was made by John W. Soule and James W. Clarke in an unpublished manuscript entitled "The New Politics and the National Conventions," but it was based

on a sample of only slightly more than one-quarter of the delegates. Their work is cited in Judith H. Parris, *The Convention Problem* (Washington, D.C.: The Brookings Institution, 1972), p. 59.

6. Sources of data on delegate experience were the following: for 1952 through 1964, Loch K. Johnson and Harlan Hahn, "Delegate Turnover at National Party Conventions, 1944–1968," in Donald R. Matthews, ed., *Perspectives on Presidential Selection* (Washington, D.C.: The Brookings Institution, 1973), p. 148; for 1968 through 1980, Mitofsky and Plissner, "Making of the Delegates," p. 43; and for 1984, Barbara G. Farah, "Delegate Polls: 1944 to 1984," *Public Opinion* 7 (August–September 1984): 44.

7. *Mandate for Reform*, pp. 46, 47–48.

8. Jeane Kirkpatrick, *The New Presidential Elite* (New York: Russell Sage Foundation and the Twentieth Century Fund, 1976), p. 48; and Austin Ranney, "The Political Parties: Reform and Decline," in Anthony King, ed., *The New American Political System* (Washington, D.C.: American Enterprise Institute, 1978), p. 233.

9. John G. Stewart, *One Last Chance* (New York: Praeger Publishers, 1974), p. 39.

10. Denis G. Sullivan, Jeffrey L. Pressman, Benjamin I. Page, and John J. Lyons, *The Politics of Representation* (New York: St. Martin's Press, 1974), p. 24.

11. Kenneth A. Bode and Carol F. Casey, "Party Reform: Revisionism Revised," in Robert A. Goldwin, ed., *Political Parties in the Eighties* (Washington, D.C., and Gambier, Ohio: American Enterprise Institute and Kenyon College, 1980), pp. 13–14.

12. Data through 1956 are from David et al., *Politics*, pp. 98, 345, 347. I compiled the data since then from the official rosters of delegates.

13. See William Crotty, *Party Reform* (New York: Longman, 1983), pp. 74–100.

14. The literature on this trend is extensive and growing. Two of the most often cited works are David R. Mayhew, *Congress: The Electoral Connection* (New Haven: Yale University Press, 1974), and Morris P. Fiorina, *Congress: Keystone of the Washington Establishment* (New Haven: Yale University Press, 1977).

15. Comments of U.S. Representative Geraldine A. Ferraro at the Conference on the Parties and the Nominating Process in December 1981, reprinted in the Republican National Committee's publication *Commonsense*, vol. 5, no. 1, p. 85. See also John F. Bibby's remarks in ibid., p. 68.

16. David et al., *Politics*, p. 375.
17. Ibid., pp. 369–376. My figures often differ from theirs (p. 371) because I used only the first ballot in multiballot conventions (for the sake of greater comparability with single-ballot conventions) and investigated states only and not nonstate areas.
18. The unit-rule states are found in ibid., p. 207; and winner-take-all states are from ibid., pp. 529–555. Alaska and Hawaii are excluded from these tables for both parties because they did not join the union until 1959.
19. Daniel J. Elazar, *American Federalism*, 2d ed. (New York: Thomas Y. Crowell Co., 1972), chap. 4. John Fenton, in a parallel to Elazar's individualistic and moralistic cultures, writes of "job-oriented" and "issue-oriented" politics, in *Midwest Politics* (New York: Holt, Rinehart & Winston, 1966).
20. See "Stalking Georgia for Teddy," *Newsweek*, January 21, 1980, p. 21.
21. Figures calculated from data provided in Kirkpatrick, *New Presidential Elite*, pp. 86, 430.
22. Unpublished analysis of 1976 Democratic delegates by CBS News. Compare their analysis of 1980 Republican delegates, which noted that Reagan delegates were as likely to be women as other delegates were, despite Reagan's problems in appealing to women voters that year.

CHAPTER 5: INTRAPARTY FACTIONALISM

1. The first part of this chapter is a revised version of my "Party Factionalism: National Conventions in the New Era," *American Politics Quarterly* 8 (July 1980): 303–318.
2. An excellent description of such conventions, written at a time when the model was becoming obsolete, is Nelson W. Polsby, "Decision-Making at the National Conventions," *Western Political Quarterly* 13 (September 1960): 609–619.
3. Earlier studies include Paul T. David, Ralph M. Goldman, and Richard C. Bain, *The Politics of National Party Conventions* (Washington, D.C.: The Brookings Institution, 1960), pp. 420–423; Richard C. Bain, *Convention Decisions and Voting Records* (Washington, D.C.: The Brookings Institution, 1960); Frank Munger and James Blackhurst, "Factionalism in the National Conventions, 1940–1964," *Journal of Politics* 27 (May 1965): 375–394; and Gerald M.

Pomper, "Factionalism in the 1968 National Conventions," *Journal of Politics* 33 (August 1971): 826–830. The only earlier study that also uses vote percentages is Anne N. Costain, "An Analysis of Voting in American National Nominating Conventions, 1940–1976," *American Politics Quarterly* 6 (January 1978): 95–120. While Costain's concerns overlap mine and she used the same definition of contested convention as I did, her method is quite different, her definitions of factions differ from mine (she treats them as though they were on the same dimension from 1940 to 1976), and she is unconcerned with how decision-making at national conventions has changed. Nevertheless, it is gratifying to see how similar her conclusions are to mine.

4. See David et al., *Politics of National Party Conventions*, pp. 420–423; and Bain, *Convention Decisions*, p. 10n.

5. Cf. Duncan MacRae Jr. and James A. Meldrum, "Critical Elections in Illinois: 1888–1958," *American Political Science Review* 54 (September 1960): 669–683.

6. Cf. David et al., *Politics of National Party Conventions*, p. 390n. The reader will recall that I have defined a contested convention as one in which more than one candidate received at least 10 percent of the vote on any ballot.

7. Bain, *Convention Decisions*.

8. Varimax rotation was used in the factor analyses; it produces highly discrete factors. The method involved principal factoring with iteration, a minimum eigenvalue of 1.0, a maximum of 25 iterations, and cessation of iteration if the successive sets of communality estimates differed by no more than .001.

9. James Q. Wilson, *The Amateur Democrat* (Chicago: University of Chicago Press, 1962).

10. Daniel J. Elazar, *American Federalism*, 2d ed. (New York: Thomas Y. Crowell Co., 1972), chap. 4. John Fenton, in a parallel to Elazar's individualistic and moralistic cultures, writes of "job-oriented" and "issue-oriented" politics in *Midwest Politics* (New York: Holt, Rinehart & Winston, 1966).

11. David et al., *Politics of National Party Conventions*, p. 207.

12. For a fuller account of recent factions among the Democrats, see my "Intra-Party Cleavages in the United States Today," *Western Political Quarterly* 34 (June 1981): 287–300.

13. Gerald M. Pomper et al., *The Election of 1976* (New York: David McKay Co., 1977), p. 26. My own view appears in "Winter Book on the GOP," *The Nation*, February 7, 1976, pp. 135–138. Although

the Republican convention of 1980 was uncontested, a delegate count shortly before the convention gave George Bush more than 10 percent of the vote; see *Congressional Quarterly Weekly Report*, June 28, 1980, p. 1801, and July 5, 1980, p. 1879. This breakdown was correlated with each of those from 1952 on and found to be significant at the .02 level or better. When it was included in the factor analysis, the result was nearly identical to that of Table 5.4. So 1980 was a continuation of this pattern.

14. David et al., in *Politics of National Party Conventions*, pp. 396–404, point out that nonstate areas behave differently from states: they are more likely to back winners, quicker to join bandwagons, and more manipulable by incumbents. I might add that they never produce candidates. Munger and Blackhurst, "Factionalism," and Pomper, "Factionalism," also exclude nonstate areas; Pomper even excluded Alaska and Hawaii from the 1960s comparisons.

15. On Sunbelt conservatism, see M. Stanton Evans, *The Future of Conservatism* (New York: Holt, Rinehart & Winston, 1968); Kevin P. Phillips, *The Emerging Republican Majority* (New Rochelle, N.Y.: Arlington House, 1969); Michael Paul Rogin and John L. Shover, *Political Change in California* (Westport, Conn.: Greenwood Publishing Corp., 1970), chap. 6; Kirkpatrick Sale, *Power Shift* (New York: Random House, 1975); and James Q. Wilson, "A Guide to Reagan Country," *Commentary*, May 1967, pp. 37–45. For a more complete statement of my view of Republican factionalism in recent years, see Reiter, "Intra-Party Cleavages."

16. For reasons given in note 14 above, nonstate areas are excluded from this analysis.

17. See Martha Wagner Weinberg, "Writing the Republican Platform," *Political Science Quarterly* 92 (Winter 1977–1978): 655–662; and Reiter, "Intra-Party Cleavages."

18. Clarke Reed, quoted in "Jostling in the GOP," *Newsweek*, May 14, 1979, p. 38.

19. V. O. Key Jr., *Politics, Parties, and Pressure Groups*, 5th ed. (New York: Thomas Y. Crowell Co., 1964), pp. 222–227.

CHAPTER 6: WHO IS NOMINATED?

1. Clinton Rossiter, *The American Presidency*, 2d ed. (New York: Harcourt, Brace & World, 1960), pp. 201–202. See also Sidney Hyman, "Nine Tests for the Presidential Hopeful," *New York Times Maga-*

zine, January 4, 1959, pp. 11, 47–50. For a nineteenth-century view, see James Bryce, *The American Commonwealth*, vol. 1 (London and New York: Macmillan, 1891), pp. 76–78.

2. Edward C. Banfield, "Party 'Reform' in Retrospect," in Robert A. Goldwin, ed., *Political Parties in the Eighties* (Washington, D.C., and Gambier, Ohio: American Enterprise Institute and Kenyon College, 1980), p. 27; William Cavala, "Changing the Rules Changes the Game," *American Political Science Review* 68 (March 1974): 40; William J. Crotty, *Decision for the Democrats* (Baltimore: Johns Hopkins University Press, 1978), pp. 255–257; Jeane Kirkpatrick, *The New Presidential Elite* (New York: Russell Sage Foundation and the Twentieth Century Fund, 1976), p. 365; idem, *Dismantling the Parties* (Washington, D.C.: American Enterprise Institute, 1978), p. 8; Judith H. Parris, *The Convention Problem* (Washington, D.C.: The Brookings Institution, 1972), p. 84; Nelson W. Polsby and Aaron Wildavsky, *Presidential Elections*, 5th ed. (New York: Charles Scribner's Sons, 1980), pp. 230–231, 238; Austin Ranney, *Curing the Mischiefs of Faction* (Berkeley: University of California Press, 1975), p. 154; and idem, "The Democratic Party's Delegate Selection Reforms, 1968–76," in Allan P. Sindler, ed., *America in the Seventies* (Boston: Little, Brown & Co., 1977), p. 195. See also the remarks of Penn Kemble, quoted in Judith A. Center, "1972 Democratic Convention Reforms and Party Democracy," *Political Science Quarterly* 89 (June 1974): 348, and those of David Broder, in Michael J. Malbin, ed., *Parties, Interest Groups, and Campaign Finance Laws* (Washington, D.C.: American Enterprise Institute, 1980), p. 327.

3. Kirkpatrick, *New Presidential Elite*, chap. 2; Polsby and Wildavsky, *Presidential Elections*, p. 82; Ranney, "Delegate Selection Reforms," p. 166; and Denis G. Sullivan, Jeffrey L. Pressman, and F. Christopher Arterton, *Explorations in Convention Decision Making* (San Francisco: W. H. Freeman & Co., 1976), p. 22.

4. See, e.g., Richard C. Bain, *Convention Decisions and Voting Records* (Washington, D.C.: The Brookings Institution, 1960), p. 287; Barton J. Bernstein, "Election of 1952," in Arthur M. Schlesinger Jr. et al., eds., *History of American Presidential Elections*, vol. 4 (New York: Chelsea House, 1971), p. 3237; and Herbert S. Parmet, *The Democrats* (New York: Macmillan, 1976), pp. 95–96, 107–108.

5. See, e.g., Clifton Brock, *Americans for Democratic Action* (Washington, D.C.: Public Affairs Press, 1962), pp. 176–178; and Arthur M. Schlesinger Jr., *A Thousand Days* (Greenwich, Conn.: Fawcett Publications, 1967), pp. 17–22.

6. Although Brown later acquired a more conservative image, especially in the wake of the passage of Proposition 13 in California in 1978, his base in 1976 was liberal. See Gary R. Orren, "Candidate Style and Voter Alignment in 1976," in Seymour Martin Lipset, ed., *Emerging Coalitions in American Politics* (San Francisco: Institute for Contemporary Studies, 1978), p. 134.

7. Arthur T. Hadley, *The Invisible Primary* (Englewood Cliffs, N.J.: Prentice-Hall, 1976), p. 278.

8. Quoted in ibid., p. 16.

9. Quoted in ibid.

10. "Dole Abandons Republican Race," *New York Times*, March 16, 1980, sec. 1, p. 30.

11. "Baker Says Campaign Survived Iowa," ibid., January 27, 1980, sec. 1, p. 16.

12. "Udall Says He Will Not Seek Presidential Nomination in 1984," ibid., February 10, 1983, p. A21.

13. Attendance records were taken from the *Congressional Quarterly Almanac* for the respective years.

14. Stephen Hess, *The Presidential Campaign*, rev. ed. (Washington, D.C.: The Brookings Institution, 1978), p. 18. "Total disaster" is a bit exaggerated. Clark was the front-runner at the 1912 Democratic convention and had a majority of the votes on seven ballots. Underwood, Johnson, and Jackson each came in second at his respective convention. Oddly enough, on page 16 Hess writes, "No longer is congressional leadership a disqualifier."

15. Rowland Evans and Robert Novak, *Lyndon B. Johnson* (New York: New American Library, 1966), chaps. 11–13.

16. *U.S. News & World Report*, January 28, 1980, p. 59. Broder's assertion is in his "Would You Prefer a Mondale-Baker Race?" *Washington Post*, June 4, 1980, p. A19.

17. "Only 6 of 18 G.O.P. Contenders Are Recognized by Half of Voters," *New York Times*, September 23, 1979, sec. 1, p. 27.

18. Jay A. Hurwitz, "Vice Presidential Eligibility and Selection Patterns," *Polity* 13 (Spring 1980): 512.

19. Paul T. David, Ralph M. Goldman, and Richard C. Bain, *The Politics of National Party Conventions* (Washington, D.C.: The Brookings Institution, 1960), p. 72.

20. *Public Papers of the Presidents of the United States: John F. Kennedy, 1963* (Washington, D.C.: Government Printing Office, 1964), p. 832.

21. Denis G. Sullivan, Jeffrey L. Pressman, Benjamin I. Page, and John J.

Lyons, *The Politics of Representation* (New York: St. Martin's Press, 1974), pp. 127–132.

22. Robert D. Novak, *The Agony of the G.O.P. 1964* (New York: Macmillan, 1965), p. 460; Stephen Shadegg, *What Happened to Goldwater?* (New York: Holt, Rinehart & Winston, 1965), p. 165; and Barry M. Goldwater, *With No Apologies* (New York: William Morrow & Co., 1979), p. 186.

23. I am of course referring to the venerable "responsible parties" debate. For the former view, see Joseph A. Schumpeter, *Capitalism, Socialism, and Democracy*, 2d ed. (New York and London: Harper & Bros., 1947), chaps. 22–23; Edward C. Banfield, "In Defense of the American Party System," in Robert A. Goldwin, ed., *Political Parties, U.S.A.* (Chicago: Rand McNally & Co., 1961), pp. 21–39; and James Q. Wilson, *The Amateur Democrat* (Chicago: University of Chicago Press, 1962), chap. 12. For the latter view, see E. E. Schattschneider, *Party Government* (New York: Rinehart & Co., 1942); "Toward a More Responsible Two-Party System," supplement to the *American Political Science Review* 44 (1950); and Stephen K. Bailey, "Our National Political Parties," in Goldwin, ed., *Political Parties, U.S.A.*, pp. 1–20.

CHAPTER 7: EFFECTS OF THE PROCESS

1. Nelson W. Polsby, *Consequences of Party Reform* (New York: Oxford University Press, 1983), pp. 140–142.

2. F. Christopher Arterton, "Recent Rules Changes Within the National Democratic Party" (Paper presented to the annual meeting of the Social Science History Association, Columbus, Ohio, November 3–5, 1978), p. 28; William Cavala, "Changing the Rules Changes the Game," *American Political Science Review* 68 (March 1974): 41–42; and James W. Ceaser, *Presidential Selection* (Princeton: Princeton University Press, 1979), pp. 296–297. I shall address the question of legitimacy in Chapter 8.

3. Denis G. Sullivan, Jeffrey L. Pressman, and F. Christopher Arterton, *Explorations in Convention Decision Making* (San Francisco: W. H. Freeman & Co., 1976), p. 119.

4. Polsby, *Consequences*, pp. 85–87.

5. Nelson W. Polsby cites data compiled by Raymond E. Wolfinger showing that the defection rate in elections to the House of Repre-

sentatives has also risen over time, from a 9–12 percent range in the 1956–1962 period to a 16–19 percent range in the 1966–1976 era. Polsby finds this increase insignificant, but I disagree, given all we know about the importance of party identification for the voter. See Polsby, "The News Media as an Alternative to Party in the Presidential Selection Process," in Robert A. Goldwin, ed., *Political Parties in the Eighties* (Washington, D.C., and Gambier, Ohio: American Enterprise Institute and Kenyon College, 1980), p. 56n.

6. *O'Brien v. Brown*, 409 U.S. 1 (1972); *Cousins v. Wigoda*, 419 U.S. 477 (1975); and *National Democratic Party v. LaFollette*, 450 U.S. 107 (1981).

7. Arterton, "Recent Rules Changes," pp. 18–22; William J. Crotty, *Decision for the Democrats* (Baltimore: Johns Hopkins University Press, 1978), pp. 257–261; John Kessel, *Presidential Campaign Politics* (Homewood, Ill.: Dorsey Press, 1980), p. 253; and Polsby, *Consequences*, pp. 78–79.

8. Ceaser, *Presidential Selection*, pp. 288–289; Jeane Kirkpatrick, *The New Presidential Elite* (New York: Russell Sage Foundation and the Twentieth Century Fund, 1976), p. 45; Gerald M. Pomper et al., *The Election of 1976* (New York: David McKay Co., 1977), p. 7; and idem, "The Decline of the Party in American Elections," *Political Science Quarterly* 92 (Spring 1977): 21–41.

9. Xandra Kayden, "The Nationalizing of the Party System," in Michael J. Malbin, ed., *Parties, Interest Groups, and Campaign Finance Laws* (Washington, D.C.: American Enterprise Institute, 1980), pp. 257–282.

10. Austin Ranney, "The Democratic Party's Delegate Selection Reforms, 1968–76," in Allan P. Sindler, ed., *America in the Seventies* (Boston: Little, Brown & Co., 1977), p. 164; and idem, "The Political Parties: Reform and Decline," in Anthony King, ed., *The New American Political System* (Washington, D.C.: American Enterprise Institute, 1978), p. 226 (emphasis in the original).

11. Quoted from Alexander Hamilton, James Madison, and John Jay, *The Federalist Papers*, ed. Clinton Rossiter (New York: New American Library, 1961), p. 244 (emphasis in the original).

12. Austin Ranney, *Curing the Mischiefs of Faction* (Berkeley: University of California Press, 1975), pp. 171–173; Ceaser, *Presidential Selection*, pp. 148–149; and in general, James S. Chase, *Emergence of the Presidential Nominating Convention 1789–1832* (Urbana: University of Illinois Press, 1972).

13. See Everett Carll Ladd Jr., *American Political Parties* (New York: W. W. Norton & Co., 1970).
14. Cornelius P. Cotter and Bernard C. Hennessy, *Politics Without Power* (New York: Atherton Press, 1964), p. 24; and Ranney, *Curing the Mischiefs*, p. 17.
15. See Ladd, *American Political Parties*.
16. Quoted in Paul T. David, Ralph M. Goldman, and Richard C. Bain, *The Politics of National Party Conventions* (Washington, D.C.: The Brookings Institution, 1960), p. 202.
17. Quoted in ibid., p. 200.
18. On the last point, see Charles D. Hadley, "The Nationalization of American Politics," *Journal of Social and Political Studies* 4 (Winter 1979): 359–380.
19. On these changes, see David et al., *Politics of Conventions*, pp. 166–169.
20. Ibid., pp. 170–173.
21. On the connection between liberalism and nationalism, see Samuel H. Beer, "Liberalism and the National Idea," *The Public Interest* 5 (Fall 1966): 70–82.
22. It is interesting to speculate about the response of liberal Democrats had a loyalty oath been proposed at the 1968 convention.
23. See Allan P. Sindler, "The Unsolid South," in Alan F. Westin, ed., *The Uses of Power* (New York: Harcourt, Brace & World, 1962), pp. 229–283; Ranney, *Curing the Mischiefs*, pp. 180–183; Cotter and Hennessy, *Politics Without Power*, pp. 32–33; Paul T. David, Malcolm Moos, and Ralph M. Goldman, *Presidential Nominating Politics in 1952* (Baltimore: Johns Hopkins University Press, 1954), vol. 1, chap. 4; and Abraham Holtzman, "Party Responsibility and Loyalty," *Journal of Politics* 22 (August 1960): 485–501.
24. Holtzman, "Party Responsibility," pp. 492 and 497n.
25. For an establishmentarian view of the controversy at the 1964 convention, see Theodore H. White, *The Making of the President 1964* (New York: Atheneum Publishers, 1965), pp. 277–282. For a black militant view, see Stokely Carmichael and Charles V. Hamilton, *Black Power* (New York: Random House, 1967), chap. 4. The perspective of one white liberal can be found in Edward N. Costikyan, *Behind Closed Doors* (New York: Harcourt, Brace & World, 1966), chap. 10.
26. Ceaser, *Presidential Selection*, pp. 257–258.
27. Donald M. Fraser, "Democratizing the Democratic Party," in Gold-

win, ed., *Parties in the Eighties*, p. 125; and Ranney, "Delegate Selection Reforms," p. 204. See also Polsby, *Consequences*, chap. 3.

28. The literature on the President and his party is remarkably scanty, but useful starting places, on which I have relied heavily, are David S. Broder, *The Party's Over* (New York: Harper & Row, 1971), pp. 1–105; and Donald Allen Robinson, "Presidents and Party Leadership" (Preliminary draft of a paper presented to the annual meeting of the American Political Science Association, Chicago, August 29–September 2, 1974). See also Robert Harmel, ed., *Presidents and Their Parties* (New York: Praeger Publishers, 1984).

29. Broder, *The Party's Over*, p. 16.

30. Robinson, "Presidents and Party Leadership," p. 21.

31. Broder, *The Party's Over*, pp. 37–39. See also Arthur M. Schlesinger Jr., *A Thousand Days* (Boston: Houghton Mifflin Co., 1965), pp. 1016, 1018; Theodore C. Sorensen, *Kennedy* (New York: Harper & Row, 1965), pp. 753–754; and Kenneth P. O'Donnell and David F. Powers, *Johnny, We Hardly Knew Ye* (New York: Pocket Books, 1973), pp. 447–448.

32. Besides Broder, *The Party's Over*, and Robinson, "Presidents and Party Leadership," see George E. Reedy, *The Twilight of the Presidency* (New York and Cleveland: World Publishing Co., 1970), pp. 61–72, 119–135. For Johnson's philosophical differences with the assumptions of party government, see Doris H. Kearns, *Lyndon Johnson and the American Dream* (New York: Signet Books, 1976), pp. 142, 148, 156–157, 161, 162–163, 253, 256, 339, 355.

33. Besides Broder, *The Party's Over*, and Robinson, "Presidents and Party Leadership," see Rowland Evans Jr. and Robert D. Novak, *Nixon in the White House* (New York: Vintage Books, 1971), pp. 28–33, 70–74, 362–364. For a fascinating portrait of White House orchestration of the 1970 Republican campaign, see William Safire, *Before the Fall* (Garden City, N.Y.: Doubleday & Co., 1975), pp. 316–326.

34. Hugh Heclo, "Presidential and Prime Ministerial Selection," in Donald R. Matthews, ed., *Perspectives on Presidential Selection* (Washington, D.C.: The Brookings Institution, 1973), pp. 45–46.

35. Edward C. Banfield, "Party 'Reform' in Retrospect," in Goldwin, ed., *Parties in the Eighties*, pp. 25, 27–28, 31.

36. Polsby, *Consequences*, p. 130.

37. Whether the electorate is indeed more ideological than it used to be is a matter of great controversy. A major argument on behalf of the

proposition can be found in Norman H. Nie, Sidney Verba, and John R. Petrocik, *The Changing American Voter* (Cambridge, Mass.: Harvard University Press, 1976).

CHAPTER 8: SOME IMPLICATIONS FOR FUTURE REFORMERS

1. Austin Ranney, "Changing the Rules of the Nominating Game," in James David Barber, ed., *Choosing the President* (Englewood Cliffs, N.J.: Prentice-Hall, 1974), p. 74; and idem, *Curing the Mischiefs of Faction* (Berkeley: University of California Press, 1975), p. 210.
2. Denis G. Sullivan, Jeffrey L. Pressman, Benjamin I. Page, and John J. Lyons, *The Politics of Representation* (New York: St. Martin's Press, 1974), pp. 35–36.
3. See Edward C. Banfield, "Party 'Reform' in Retrospect," in Robert A. Goldwin, ed., *Political Parties in the Eighties* (Washington, D.C., and Gambier, Ohio: American Enterprise Institute and Kenyon College, 1980), pp. 20–33; and, in the same volume, Banfield's "In Defense of the American Party System," pp. 133–149. A typically extreme expression of the general viewpoint is that of Irving Kristol: "I have observed over the years that the unanticipated consequences of social action are *always* more important, and usually less agreeable, than the intended consequences" (emphasis added). Irving Kristol, *On the Democratic Idea in America* (New York: Harper & Row, 1972), p. ix.
4. David S. Broder, "Would You Prefer a Mondale-Baker Race?" *Washington Post*, June 4, 1980, p. A19.
5. James W. Ceaser, "Political Change and Party Reform," in Goldwin, ed., *Parties in the Eighties*, pp. 110, 114.
6. Denis G. Sullivan, Jeffrey L. Pressman, and F. Christopher Arterton, *Explorations in Convention Decision Making* (San Francisco: W. H. Freeman & Co., 1976), pp. 124–126.
7. See his remarks in Michael J. Malbin, ed., *Parties, Interest Groups, and Campaign Finance Laws* (Washington, D.C.: American Enterprise Institute, 1980), p. 315. Cf., in another context: "By focusing on the breakdown as the author of our woes, one holds out the hope that all can be well again if only it can be repaired; by stressing the cause of the breakdown, a revolutionary process that has been going on for some centuries, one knows that the revival of the old *Gemeinschaft* is impossible" (Michael Harrington, *The Twilight of*

Capitalism [New York: Simon & Schuster, 1976], p. 290).

8. William Chapman, "Democratic Reforms Would Boost 'Ins,'" *Washington Post*, April 27, 1973, p. A19.
9. David S. Broder, "Campaign Shortages," *Washington Post*, June 15, 1980, p. D7; and Laurence Radway, "The Curse of Free Elections," *Foreign Policy* 40 (Fall 1980): 73.
10. Everett Carll Ladd, "A Better Way to Pick Our Presidents," *Fortune*, May 5, 1980, pp. 135–138.
11. The proposal can be found in an undated photocopied manuscript entitled simply "Hunt Commission Report," pp. 6 and 15–18 of the report and pp. 13–17 of the rules proposals. On the report, see Adam Clymer, "Democrats Alter Delegate Rules, Giving Top Officials More Power," *New York Times*, March 27, 1982, pp. 1, 10; and Rhodes Cook, "Democrats' Rules Weaken Representation," *Congressional Quarterly Weekly Report*, April 3, 1982, pp. 749–751.
12. Quoted from Alexander Hamilton, James Madison, and John Jay, *The Federalist Papers*, ed. by Clinton Rossiter (New York: New American Library, 1961), pp. 342, 360. See also A. Lawrence Lowell, *Public Opinion and Popular Government* (New York: Johnson Reprint Corp., 1969), p. 140. On the size of conventions, see Paul T. David, Ralph M. Goldman, and Richard C. Bain, *The Politics of National Party Conventions* (Washington, D.C.: The Brookings Institution, 1960), pp. 213–217; Judith H. Parris, *The Convention Problem* (Washington, D.C.: The Brookings Institution, 1972), pp. 86–96; and Stephen J. Wayne, *The Road to the White House* (New York: St. Martin's Press, 1980), pp. 116–117.
13. Woodrow Wilson, *Constitutional Government in the United States* (New York: Columbia University Press, 1961), p. 61. See also James Bryce, *The American Commonwealth*, vol. 2 (London and New York: Macmillan, 1891), pp. 183–195; and M. Ostrogorski, *Democracy and the Organization of Political Parties*, vol. 2 (New York: Haskell House Publishers, 1970), pp. 278–279.
14. Bryce, *American Commonwealth*, 2:180. See also Ostrogorski, *Democracy*, 2:87; Woodrow Wilson, "Leaderless Government," in Ray Stannard Baker and William E. Dodd, eds., *The Public Papers of Woodrow Wilson*, vol. 1 (New York: Harper & Bros., 1925), pp. 344–345; and Edward McChesney Sait, *American Parties and Elections*, 3d ed. (New York: D. Appleton-Century Co., 1942), p. 578.
15. Kenneth A. Bode and Carol F. Casey, "Party Reform: Revisionism Revised," in Goldwin, ed., *Parties in the Eighties*, p. 15.

16. Moreover, a Gallup press release dated March 9, 1980, showed Ronald Reagan running better against Jimmy Carter than was George Bush, who was supported by many party leaders. See Chapter 3.
17. See James W. Davis, *Presidential Primaries* (New York: Thomas Y. Crowell Co., 1967), chap. 4; and James R. Beniger, "Winning the Presidential Nomination," *Public Opinion Quarterly* 40 (Spring 1976): 34–36. For a contrary view, see William H. Lucy, "Polls, Primaries, and Presidential Nominations," *Journal of Politics* 35 (November 1973): 839.
18. Sullivan et al., *Politics of Representation*, p. 111.
19. Data graciously provided by Carey Funk of CBS News.
20. See the comments of John F. Bibby and U. S. Representative Geraldine A. Ferraro at the Conference on the Parties and the Nominating Process in December 1981, reprinted in the Republican National Committee's publication *Commonsense*, vol. 5, no. 1, pp. 68, 85. See also Robert Shogan, "The Gap: Why Presidents and Parties Fail," *Public Opinion* 5 (August–September 1982): 19. My skepticism is shared by Nelson Polsby, in his *Consequences of Party Reform* (New York: Oxford University Press, 1983), p. 175, and by Byron E. Shafer in his *Quiet Revolution* (New York: Russell Sage Foundation, 1983), p. 537.
21. See Polsby, *Consequences*, p. 178.
22. George McGovern, "The Democrats Change the Rules," *The Nation*, May 15, 1982, pp. 580–582. See also the sources in note 11, above.
23. See, e.g., Ranney, "Changing the Rules," pp. 73–74.
24. A comprehensive treatment of the subject is Hanna Fenichel Pitkin, *The Concept of Representation* (Berkeley: University of California Press, 1967).
25. *Bode v. National Democratic Party*, 452 F.2d 1302 (D.C. Cir. 1971); *Georgia v. National Democratic Party*, 447 F.2d 1271, 1275 (D.C. Cir. 1971); and *Ripon Society, Inc., v. National Republican Party*, 525 F.2d 548, 567 (D.C. Cir. 1975).
26. *Buckley v. Valeo*, 424 U.S. 1 (1976).
27. *O'Brien v. Brown*, 409 U.S. 1 (1972); *Cousins v. Wigoda*, 419 U.S. 477 (1975); and *National Democratic Party v. LaFollette*, 450 U.S. 107 (1981).
28. *Columbia Broadcasting System v. Federal Communications Commission*, 453 U.S. 367 (1981).

29. William F. Buckley Jr., "His Unbiased Analysis," *Norwich Bulletin* (Connecticut), August 7, 1980, p. 6.
30. Everett Carll Ladd Jr., *Where Have All the Voters Gone?* (New York: W. W. Norton & Co., 1978), p. 59. See also Penn Kemble and Josh Muravchik, "The New Politics and the Democrats," *Commentary*, December 1972, pp. 78–84; Jeane Kirkpatrick, *The New Presidential Elite* (New York: Russell Sage Foundation and the Twentieth Century Fund, 1976); and Shafer, *Quiet Revolution*, Conclusion.
31. James Q. Wilson, *The Amateur Democrat* (Chicago: University of Chicago Press, 1962).
32. Theodore J. Lowi, *Incomplete Conquest*, 2d ed. (New York: Holt, Rinehart & Winston, 1981), p. 481. From the context it is plain that Lowi is emphasizing the changes since 1968, for on the same page he cites the proliferation of primaries as "the most fundamental change in the politics of the presidency in the twentieth century." See also his more general remarks in *The End of Liberalism* (New York: W. W. Norton & Co., 1969), pp. 93–97.

Index